Daily Rebellion

Cover design by: Sara Young
Cover photo by: Andrew van Tilborgh

ISBN: 978-1-964794-52-5   1 2 3 4 5 6 7 8 9 10

Printed in the United States of America

"Being a talented, busy, and successful Christian isn't the same as being in sync with God—and nobody models this better than Kevin Taylor. *Daily Rebellion* offers a wide range of practical solutions for how we can reconnect with God and avoid the chaos of the world. Kevin Taylor gently presses on all the sore spots in your soul and sweetly calls you back to the voice of the Father. I sighed out of conviction so many times in one chapter that my wife demanded I read the whole thing to her! I can promise you: this book will reconnect your soul to heaven."

—Peter Haas
Pastor of SubstanceChurch.com
Author of *Broken Escalators: The Counterintuitive Art* and *Science of Happiness*

"*Daily Rebellion* is a timely, authentic, and practical guide for anyone longing to reconnect with God in the chaos of modern life. With humor, Biblical depth, and actionable soul-care practices, Kevin Taylor offers more than inspiration—he provides a wise and relatable companion for the journey toward true biblical rest."

—John Zick
National Director of Ministerial
Advancement, Assemblies of God USA

"In over four decades of ministry, I've encountered countless books championing church growth and leadership strategies—but precious few that speak directly to the soul of the leader. *Daily Rebellion* by Kevin Taylor is a rare and vital exception. This book is not just a devotional—it's a defiant act of grace. It dares to confront the noise, the pace, and the addiction to activity that so often leaves leaders burnt out and spiritually hollow. Kevin's words offer a countercultural call to reclaim sacred slowness, restore holy rhythms, and recover the soul beneath the title. In my view, this is one of the most significant contributions to the health and longevity of Christian leaders in the past decade. Read it. Live it. And join the rebellion—one pause, one breath, one soul-sabbath at a time."

—Michael Murphy
Co-Founder Leaderscape
Chancellor Alphacrucis University College

"In a world that glorifies hustle, this book is a Spirit-breathed invitation to stop, breathe, and reconnect with what matters most—your soul. Kevin doesn't just offer good advice; he offers a lifeline, rooted in Scripture and shaped by his own vulnerable journey. I personally have struggled with slowing down and simply pausing, but I discovered in *Daily Rebellion* how 'pressing pause' can transform my life! Read this book slowly, reflect deeply, and let the Holy Spirit use these pages to restore your joy, peace, and purpose."

—Rob Ketterling
Lead Pastor of River Valley Church
in Minneapolis, Minnesota

"*Daily Rebellion* felt like a deep breath in a world full of noise. I meant to read a little, then rest. Instead, I devoured it and forgot to breathe. That's how good this book is—and how deeply it speaks to our need for real rest."

—Ty Buckingham
Evangelist and Author

"In today's hectic and distracting pace of life, Kevin Taylor's life-changing book is especially timely. Written from deep personal and spiritual experience, he invites us to join his journey to a more effective life, stronger faith, and greater peace."

—Randy Hurst
Assemblies of God missionary

"Daily Rebellion is a book I needed. From the title to the final page, I love Kevin Taylor's choice of wording, imagery and storytelling, all of which invite the reader to take a deep breath. The prompts and tools inside incorporate that kind of 'pause' and reset, as regular rhythms to life. If you are like me, my gut is that you are too busy NOT to read this book."

—Paul Hurckman
Executive Director, Venture

"This book doesn't just talk about rest—it hits different. It's real, raw, and soul-level honest, like a deep breath for folks running on fumes. In a world that keeps us grinding, *Daily Rebellion* shows us how to stop, breathe, and actually live."

—Bishop Walter Harvey
President, the WI+H Movement

"Daily Rebellion should be required reading for every Christian Leader. Kevin Taylor has masterfully blended brilliant storytelling, rich theological truths, and his very honest pastoral heart to present a book that so humbly calls us back to a place of increased devotion to our Lord. Deeply convicting and challenging, this is one of those books you will finish, wishing you'd read it years earlier."

—Pastor Mike Burnette
LifePoint Church, Clarksville, Tennessee

Daily Rebellion

The Everyday Fight to Press Pause

Includes 60-minute practices to quiet the noise and strengthen your soul.

Kevin S. Taylor

AVAIL

Contents

Acknowledgments

I t has been a bucket list goal and dream of mine to write a book. I wasn't sure I could do it. Others believed differently. To each of them I owe thanks.

To Joelene, whom I adore, thank you for being my partner in life for more than forty-four years. Inside these pages you let me share a small part of our wonderful life together. I trust that you were honored in the mutual memories I chose. Your mark of Jesus devotion impacts me every day. You are the greatest person I know—and you are the only person who gets all my jokes. LoVE.

To my beloved inner circle—daughters Whitney, Allison, and Olivia—thank you for your unwavering support and unquestioning belief that I could complete this task and make a difference because of it. I am grateful for your brands of wisdom that advised me from start to finish.

To my sons-in-law—Darren and Brandyn—thanks for being a strength in the background of this journey. Darren, your particular insight into the business of it all was indispensable.

To my six Grankies—Elias, Ruby, Tessa, Calvin, Jenson, and Hayden—thank you for allowing me to use each of your names in various stories included here. I didn't ask you, I just did it, but it was out of intense G-pa love for you. You are each my pride and joy.

To my one and only mom, you are the best. I can do no wrong in your eyes, and you have always imagined I was bigger and greater than my reality. Today, I almost feel you were right.

To so many of the team at the church I love and serve, your "Let's go" was and is a soaring banner. You put courage into me, and your willingness to be my "daily rebellion guinea pigs" is appreciated. Your presence in my life is fuel and a continual gift.

To my soul family, Journey Church, I trust I have made you proud. My heart is devoted to you. Thank you for your ongoing love and prayers. I owe so much to each of you.

To my ministry friends, mentors, and spiritual guides who read these pages before the consumer did—some of you authors in your own right—your encouragement, thumbs up, and suggestions to be better was everything. If I don't end up a bestselling author like each of you, it's totally your fault.

To Pete Fisher, your passion for personal soul care and the things of Jesus have perhaps been the greatest earthly inspiration for this work. I barely knew a thing about soul care before I met you. Each year at the Silent Prayer Retreat in Waupaca, Wisconsin, your hunger and genuineness for Jesus kept me coming back over and again. You taught me by your own life not only how to care for my soul, but how to cherish it. You are a true Jesus rebel.

To Martijn at AVAIL and Megan, my coach and editor, your leadership and guidance through this process was invaluable. Thank you for the opportunity and for catching things I missed, advising best practices, and spurring me on with praise that I wasn't always convinced was for real, but it sure did keep me going.

To the readers, seekers, and souls who will hold this book—it was written for you. May these pages feel like a warm cup in your hands, a soft place to land, and a gentle provocation to pause and rebel.

And to every difficult moment, every dark night, and every quiet breakthrough that shaped these pages—you were not the end, you were the beginning—the hidden teachers.

With a full heart to the God I love, my Creator and the Divine Source of peace, healing, and restoration, I thank You above all. You whispered stillness into my chaos. You met me in thousands of moments of silence, and You stayed. May every word reflect my sacred connection with You.

Introduction

I think I might be allergic to stillness. Or maybe I'm just highly motivated by movement.

The moment I sit down—BAM!—my right leg starts bouncing like a jackhammer. Not my left one . . . my right one. It is a monster with a mind of its own, as if it decided to burn extra calories without the consent of the rest of me. It rebels against stillness.

I checked my phone fifteen seconds ago, but here I go checking it again. I continue refreshing the screen every couple of minutes, like I'm expecting breaking news about my own existence. My brain has convinced me that something amazing is waiting for me right around the corner. It's critical that I check. One more refresh won't hurt. Swipe. My thumb needs counseling.

My mind is a browser with eighty-two open tabs:

Should I adjust my schedule for tomorrow?

Did I remember to reply to that last text?

I really want a puppy.

What's for dinner?

Did Adam have a belly button?

What is the meaning of life?

Is the Loch Ness monster real?

Who decided the alphabet should be in that order?

I need a pause button for my brain.

If there's a pen available, I'll click it. It starts innocently enough. A casual, single click. A tiny, harmless motion of my other thumb. Both thumbs are now complicit. Before I know it, I'm in a deep and symphonic rhythm, clicking away like I'm transmitting Morse Code. I tell myself just one more click, then I'm done. But I go again.

Click-click. Click-click.

It soon becomes an unconscious action. Without realizing, I'm gripping the pen like a detonator, unable to resist the next satisfying snap of the plastic.

Click-click. Click-click.

The room notices, though I'm still unaware. George Meyer said, "The most oblivious people are often the happiest."[1] Let's go with that. Someone across the table gives me the side-eye. I don't know why. I continue clicking. A

---

[1] George Meyer, interview by Eric Spitznagel, The Believer, September 1, 2004, https://www.believermag.com/issues/200409/?read=interview_meyer.

coworker clears his throat. I keep on. My brain refuses to process that I am the source of their irritation.

Click-click. Click-click.

Had my wife been sitting anywhere near, she would have never let it get this far. She would have reached over and calmly but firmly put her hand on my leg under the table. I know that signal. It's hardly subtle. *Be still, Kevin.* She doesn't actually say the words; she doesn't need to. She's a one-click woman.

Click...

It's hard to pause and be still. Everything around me is moving so fast, it feels like rebellion to act, be, or think otherwise.

This book is about soul care—not as a luxury, but as a daily act of rebellion.

Rebellion sounds like a dirty word. For many, it conjures images of chaos, defiance, pushing back against authority. It can feel and be dangerous, unruly, even sinful. But not all rebellion is created equal.

The Patriots against the British in the American Revolution . . . human rights advocates of the Civil Rights movement . . . the Berlin Wall protesters who ultimately brought the wall down . . . the Rebel Alliance vs. the Galactic Empire in the *Star Wars* trilogy (sorry, couldn't resist) . . . rebellions, all.

There is a holy kind of rebellion—a rebellion that resists what is wrong in favor of what is right. Not rebellion against God, but a rebellion of the soul.

Jesus Himself was a kind of rebel—not because He sought disorder, but because He brought a radically different kind of order.

He healed on the Sabbath.

He touched untouchables.

He walked away from crowds.

He paused when others refused to.

He didn't rebel against truth. He rebelled against everything that kept people from it.

So, no, rebellion doesn't have to be a dirty word. Sometimes, rebellion is the most sacred thing you can do. It's the intentional turning of your attention inward and upward. It's listening for the whisper of God when everything else demands your urgency. It's pausing not because you've earned it, but because you're human and you need it.

In choosing to care for your soul; you are actively resisting the lie that your worth is tied to your output. You're rejecting the constant tug of distraction, weightiness, and fear. You're saying no to the world's rhythm—and yes to God's.

That is rebellion.

Rebellion doesn't have to be loud or flashy. It can actually be quiet and gentle. But make no mistake—it's powerful. Each time you pause to sit in silence, to pray with honesty, or to simply rest and listen, you are protesting a culture that's forgotten how to celebrate those things and revel in them.

Meaningful, life-giving, rebellious pauses can be as simple as:

A deep breath before moving from one assignment to the next.

A moment of gratitude before starting or ending your day.

A short walk outside to clear your mind.

A break from screens to reconnect with the present.

A day... or an evening... or an hour of peace without shame.

Imagine you're holding a large glass full of water. At first it's light, easy to carry. But as minutes stretch into hours, the weight doesn't change—yet it feels heavier. Your wrist starts to ache. You feel your grip beginning to weaken. If you don't put the glass down, eventually it will slip from your hand and shatter on the floor.

We each carry the weight of responsibility, expectations, schedules, checklists and live in a world of constant noise. At first, we tell ourselves we can handle it. We push through. We ignore the tension growing in our spirit, feel the exhaustion creeping in. Over time, the weight becomes unbearable. If we never lay it down—never give ourselves permission to lay it down—something inside us starts to crack.

This book is about setting the glass down and learning to pause. It's making the choice to listen instead of rush, to reflect instead of react, to breathe out instead of burn out, to live a version of rebellion that God sees as faith.

As you read, you'll find practical ways to integrate pauses into your daily life and biblical exercises to center your life and soul around. You will find how to use these pauses to hear God's voice more clearly and reconnect with what and who truly matters.

In the pages that follow, you will discover:

» How "soul pauses" are biblical pauses
» The power of pausing to understand who God is and who you are
» The connection between pausing, abiding, and surrendering
» How the Holy Spirit is involved in pausing
» How to pause to listen and remember
» The beauty of pausing outdoors
» The necessity of pausing to connect with others
» Why pausing to be grateful matters
» What to do when you're forced to pause

. . . At the end of each chapter, you'll find a hack to help you pause and some thoughtful reflections and applications that will help you put it all into practice.

The pages that follow aren't about being still for the sake of it. They're about making space for what really matters—about finding clarity, rediscovering joy and fulfillment, and aligning our hearts and actions with God-values.

I may not know you personally, but I know this is what your soul craves. As you read, don't read the way you've read the last twenty books. Read more slowly. Stop and ponder throughout. Have a pen at the ready. Accept this invitation to pause and prioritize the care of the most important thing about you—your soul. Because sometimes the most profound progress begins with a simple pause.

Now, before you turn the page, take a moment to get started.

Still your leg. Stop the click. Put the glass down. Close your eyes. Inhale deeply. Exhale slowly. Invite Jesus in. This sacred and simple pause is where your journey back to presence starts.

Let the rebellion begin.

Chapter 1

Here the Rebellion Began

"You cannot be a true rebel unless you are also deeply rooted in something you love."
—Clarissa Pinkola Estes[2]

The first time I attended a silent prayer retreat in Waupaca, Wisconsin—which changed my life—was by invitation from a good friend, one of the pastors on our church team.

We agreed to drive together on a Sunday three hours north to the campground where the retreat was held, but we couldn't get there until very late due to an important

---

2   Clarissa Pinkola Estes, *Women Who Run with the Wolves: Myths and Stories of the Wild Woman Archetype* (New York, NY: Ballatine Books, 1996), 217.

meeting at our church that evening. That meant we would miss the opening gathering, the initial explanations for the retreat, the handing out of retreat materials, not to mention the important last opportunity to chat with the other participants before they rang the "no talking" bell that would last for the next three days.

Though I had never been, I knew that silent . . . meant silent. At meals. At the teaching times. All during the day and night. No talking. Phone service was sketchy-to-nonexistent there—not a bad crutch to give up when the goal is to pause and feed your soul, but not an inviting proposition for a guy who wants to stay connected to the world.

We arrived Sunday around midnight. By previous arrangement, our lodging was designated and retreat materials laid on the beds in our private rooms. Before dropping off, I scanned the notebook to get a feel for the schedule that resumed early Monday morning. See what I had signed up for.

Breakfast was at 7:30 a.m. I had already been assigned a seat in the dining hall for meals as well as in the retreat center for the three-times-a-day short teachings. These sessions broke up the hours alone spent with Jesus and provided direction for those times, if needed. The advance seating was designed to remove unnecessary choices so your heart, brain, mind, and soul could focus on Jesus. No debating who to sit by, no extraneous decisions to make. The concept was centered around decision fatigue—the idea that making too many choices drains mental energy and leaves you with less focus. Steve Jobs had made a habit of wearing the same thing every day to avoid wasting energy on things he considered trivial. If it worked for Steve Jobs …

It was a crisp October morning on the way from my room to the dining hall for my first meal. I noticed a man walking ahead of me, head down, hands in pockets, shuffling along. I came up on him quickly, like a Maserati overtaking a Citroen on the Autobahn. He was walking as if his feet were slogging through quicksand. Were he walking any slower he would have been going backward. I effortlessly breezed past, my arms swinging freely in the brisk of the a.m.

As I opened the door to the hall, it felt like I had entered a time capsule. The whole room was moving in slow motion. It was not a mirage, and I was not experiencing an out-of-body moment; it was reality. Everyone was moving at the speed of sloth, all eyes to the ground like monks in training. I knew many of these folks personally and yet they would not look me in the eye.

It was not what I expected nor what I bargained for. But for the remainder of the retreat, I adopted a "when in Rome" philosophy. Eyes down. Lots of slogging. If a hundred people are doing it, it must be right.

I discovered that slowing my pace and lowering my eyes did a lot of things, most of them good. I will admit I bumped into a few things at first. Until I got the hang of it. But slowing down sharpened my thought processes. Relaxed my body. Lowered my anxiety levels. Increased my mindfulness and my ability to better sense things around me. Detached me from the demands of everyday life. Improved my focus and concentration. Intensified my spiritual antenna to hear the voice of God.

For starters.

The pausing in order to be still delivered. I did hear His voice. It was real. It was clear—as close to an audible as I've ever experienced.

IIIIIIIIIIIIIIIIIIIIIIIIIIIIIIIIIIIIIIIIIIIIIIIIIIIIIIIIIIIIIIIIIIIIIIIIIIIIIIIIIIIIIIIIIII

There's a hole—if not on the soul-care shelf at the library, then in our hearts.

IIIIIIIIIIIIIIIIIIIIIIIIIIIIIIIIIIIIIIIIIIIIIIIIIIIIIIIIIIIIIIIIIIIIIIIIIIIIIIIIIIIIIIIIIII

After only three days, I was completely sold on the pause, and I haven't missed a silent prayer retreat since— and our staff soul-care days were born (more on that in a later chapter).

This book owes its birth to that retreat.

It's been years since that time, but it stirred an internal passion that I had not known was there. It evolved through a growing awareness that my soul needed something more of Jesus than I currently had. I needed Him during the long nights of brokenness and spiritual boredom—but just as much during periods of spiritual excitement—and in all of it, the beautiful discovery that every decision that led to stillness over striving was a quiet rebellion that defied the chaos that threatened to own me.

Before I began to labor on this work, I Googled "books on soul care" and ended up scrolling for a solid ten minutes. The scroll ended up being an encouragement—a signal—for me to add my voice. The thirst to be connected to God is great.

There's a hole—if not on the soul-care shelf at the library, then in our hearts.

As much as this is my story, it's really our story—the story of every person who longs to live a life of purpose, shalom, and divine connection—to acknowledge the need to rebel and press pause and not feel guilty about it—to turn inward and open ourselves to the sacred. When we do, life that is truly life comes to life. We become more like the disciples Jesus marked us to be.

Natural Pauses

Admittedly, it's daunting to think about pausing when life is packed with kids, errands, work and responsibilities, but even small moments of stillness can make a difference. Fortunately, you don't have to attend a three-day retreat to experience the beauty and rebellion of pausing.

Actually, you're already pausing—you just don't know you are.

You grab the remote and freeze media content in order to take a quick break, to handle something important (or trivial) without missing anything, or rewind to catch what you missed.

I have a friend who is famous for this. We'll be watching a movie, and he'll say, "Hold on. Can you press pause?"

"Why?"

"I need to see that again."

A pause and a rewind every now and then are totally acceptable. Everybody needs a take two every once in a while. But asking to pause a movie four times because you weren't paying attention again . . . and again . . . and again? Come on!

He might say, "Let's press pause, so we can microwave some popcorn."

"Okay. Can we not call a pause right when the car chase is in mid-air?"

And: "My phone is ringing. Press pause for a minute."

Agggghh!!!

Since the 2020 Zoom revolution, we've become comfortable with pausing our audio and video to covertly step away from an online audience for a personal break or to shove some yogurt into our mouths when no one can see.

We press pause by shutting the office door for a quick power nap in the middle of the day.

We retreat to the bathroom, not because we have to use it for what it was intended, but because we know it's a safe hideout for a few moments of peace.

Taking the long route somewhere can be a way to press pause—that extra twenty minutes helps us reclaim the day.

We press pause by standing in the shower and letting the water cascade down our bodies. We reflect on life in that little wet cubicle, we win imaginary arguments and accept potential Grammy awards there.

There's a natural pause between every inhale and exhale throughout the day. We don't even notice this pause, yet we engage it hundreds of times in a 24-hour period.

According to Nationwide Insurance, "Life comes at you fast." The world drives us to keep going, keep working, keep producing. The moment we slow down, guilt moves in, as if to suggest that stillness is a sign of weakness, and rest is something to be earned rather than enjoyed.

But what if we've been viewing it all wrong? What if pausing isn't a disruption, but a doorway into beautiful and godly rebellion?

Composers understand this. Truman Fisher said, "The pause is as important as the note."[3] Claude Debussy, "Music is the space between the notes."[4] The melody isn't just shaped by the notes played, but by the spaces between them—the rests. They are as much a part of the music as the tune. Those pauses aren't an absence of music; they're what gives music texture and meaning.

But unlike a symphonic composition that needs the pause to exist, we often resist the pause. We fill every gap in our schedules, crowd out every moment of silence, and our hands constantly hover over the iPhones cradled in our unsnapped holsters. Stillness feels unnatural in a culture that glorifies the frenetic.

When we live without natural pauses, we move from one thing to the next without stopping long enough to ask:

---

3   Barry, quote on pausing, *The Quotable Coach,* accessed June 20, 2025, https://www.thequotablecoach.com/the-pause-is-as-important-as-the-note/.
4   Corinna da Fonseca-Wollheim, "How the Silence Makes the Music," *The New York Times,* 2 Oct. 2019, https://www.nytimes.com/2019/10/02/arts/music/silence-classical-music.html.

"Am I living in harmony with what matters most? Do I even know what matters most? Is my soul thriving?"

What often results is a life running on empty, chasing the next hopeful silver bullet that will be the answer to life abundant.

Failing to Press Pause

There was a time in my life when I believed I had everything figured out. That happens most often when you're under thirty-five years old. Since I've always been something of a late bloomer, at forty-five, I still thought I was pretty much invincible.

My family has a history of long life. As of this writing, my mother is eighty-eight years old and going strong. My dad died at ninety, and my maternal grandmother was ninety-six when she passed. Her mother, my great-grandmother, was a few months short of 110 on her last day, the oldest person in the state of Missouri at that time. I've told my wife, "Get used to me because I'm never going to die."

Things were going well. I was building my ministry while caring for and leading my wife and three teenage daughters, checking off all the things I thought success—with work, ministry, home life, and a walk with Jesus—should look like.

Contrary to conventional wisdom that pastors work one day a week—on Sundays—ministry can be challenging. Resources can be limited, relationships get strained, people want more than you have the capacity to give, and the wisdom you're asked to dish out comes up short. The number of people who call your church "home base" is the number of bosses to whom you are accountable. Isolation increases. Family life can become compromised.

You're expected to be an expert at:

- » visioning
- » finances
- » construction
- » decorating and designing
- » counseling
- » conflict resolution
- » time management
- » problem identification and problem solving
- » stage communication
- » team building
- » project management
- » fundraising
- » delegation
- » developing people
- » funerals and weddings
- » visitation and pastoral care
- » consulting and coaching

And it doesn't hurt if you can make a decent macchiato in your office for guests.

To be fair, ministry has a ton of upside and fulfilling rewards. Nevertheless, it isn't a job; it's a calling. Romans 11 says, "The gifts and calling of God are without repentance" (v. 29, KJV), which I think means, if you don't like it, you can't blame God for it.

But for a good twenty-plus years, things seemed to be going great—people liked me, the work was headed up and to the right, and I had a promising future, favor with my boss, and affirmation from onlookers. On the outside, everything was beautiful. But on the inside, I found myself...

...spiritually exhausted

...unable to summon the emotional strength to walk through my front door some nights

...finding it more and more challenging to be driven by joy

...doing a lot of work for Jesus but failing to do it in the strength of the Holy Spirit

On top of all that, we found ourselves in an economic crisis almost overnight. We had built a home and lived in it happily for ten years. After that length of time, we decided to do it again. This move would set us up with a positive financial future and would fulfill another family dream we had long imagined.

So, we made a plan to build a new house.

I remember the day the excavating equipment rolled onto our new, forested, one-acre plot of land, creating a gaping hole where the foundation of the house would sit.

It was 2008. Remember 2008?

The bottom dropped out of—well—everything. The most devastating global economic crisis since the Great Depression. Home foreclosures. Savings accounts, retirement funds, and personal net worth ransacked. Stock market decline. Unemployment highs. The failure of banks and financial institutions around the world. Balloons popping everywhere.

And the well-meaning but unfortunate Taylors were selling a home and building a home. (My youngest daughter has often said to me, "Dad, the one thing I inherited from you is that I'm unfortunate." She isn't wrong.)

With the failure to offload our first home short of accepting quarters on the dollar and eventually having to drain equity from house #1 (that we still owed on) to pay the mortgage and taxes and utility bills on house #2 (a situation that lasted more than eighteen months), I began to see our financial future evaporating before my eyes, multiplying my anxiety and despair. Compounded by doing ministry in my own strength while floating down a spiritually dry stream bed, real life came into view.

It was during this season that I reached rock bottom, never dreaming I could dive so headlong into despondency. That kind of thing happened to other people—dysfunctional, defective, wounded people—not me.

On a cold, dreary November afternoon that only encouraged the sentiments roiling in my spirit to the surface, I found myself sitting in my car in the garage of house #2, depleted of hope. What was I going to do? What were WE going to do? With one push of a button, the garage door lowered behind me, and with the car engine still running, the thought flickered, *I wonder how long this takes?*

It was fleeting—a whisper, really. I instantly recognized the source of it. The deceiver, my enemy, the prowling lion, the chief of liars, the accuser was baiting me. The thought disappeared in the next instant; nevertheless, it had been there.

I questioned my sanity to find myself at such an explosive place. If my church ever found out these kinds of thoughts were invading my brain even for one moment, what would they say? I knew it was something I could not admit out loud. It wasn't acceptable for a man-of-the-cloth to be entertaining something like this even for one second. Take every thought captive—think on things that are good—be transformed by the renewing of your mind. I knew the drill.

||||||||||||||||||||||||||||||||||||||||||||||||||||||||||||||||||||||||||||||

Everybody needs to find a reason and a way to press pause for the sake of their soul.

||||||||||||||||||||||||||||||||||||||||||||||||||||||||||||||||||||||||||||||

I stared at the steering wheel, hands gripped at ten and two, tears streaming down my face, and thought, *There has to be more to life than this. This isn't what matters most. Right?*

That moment was a wake-up call, sudden and tangible. The most important part of me was sick. So focused on doing good things and living on an upward trajectory, I had forgotten how to be. I was faithful to share the gospel every weekend to a couple of thousand people, but my own soul wasn't listening. My inner life was screaming for attention, and now my outer life was following suit. That night, I eked out a simple, desperate plea: "God, I can't do this. I need

You. Show me how to hear You. Feel You. See You. Show me how to begin again."

That journey restarted slowly, one step at a time—some steps so small, I was certain they were imagined. I began carving out short moments of stillness in my day—a minute pause here, a five-minute pause there—to simply, and as purely as I knew how, sit with God for a moment, saying little. Just being aware of Him. I began to journal certain thoughts and prayers, letting the pages hold things I couldn't bring myself to say to another human.

Gradually, a weight began to lift. My soul began to feel a hint of what "alive" might mean once again. It wasn't until some years later at that silent prayer retreat that I began to organize my thoughts and heart around truly caring for my own soul in some kind of systematic, yet life-giving, way.

I share this part of my story because I know I'm not alone. Everybody has moments, days, and seasons of weariness, carrying weights not meant for them. Everybody needs to find a reason and a way to press pause for the sake of their soul.

The beautiful thing is, Jesus showed us how. He recognized the importance of pauses and modeled them—not only everyday regular pauses but sacred, life-giving ones.

What Is It?

We use the word "soul" casually in a variety of situations and settings:

- » She bared her soul to me.
- » He puts his heart and soul into his hobby.

» They found their perfect soul mate in each other.
» After the breakup, she took time to do some soul-searching.
» You can tell him anything; he's the soul of discretion.
» The music was soul-stirring; it brought tears to my eyes.
» Her homemade beans and collards are pure soul food.

These idioms help us understand that we have a soul in there somewhere, yet it continues to be something of an enigma. Who we are is a mystery—even to ourselves.

We understand our bodies. They relate to the parts we can see and touch. Created by God from the dust of the ground, your body is your temple—the shell the Spirit of God inhabits. The body doesn't live forever. You know this if you aren't a teenager. It's wasting away. You are annoyingly mortal. Things sag where they shouldn't. Parts creak and groan without apology. Joints scream at you with no mercy. Lines appear where just yesterday skin was smooth as a baby's . . . well, you know.

But good news about your body—it will be renewed and transformed one day at the resurrection (1 Corinthians 15:42-44).

Amen. Can't wait.

You also have an inner being that's less understood. The inner you has intrigued humanity for millennia. But it is an integral part of human identity and dignity.

The soul is the life center of human beings.[5] It is the capacity to integrate all the parts into a single whole life.[6] It is the gathering place for your emotions, intellect, will, and personality. Your Enneagram number and DISC letter are in there somewhere. It encompasses your one-and-only you-and-only-you identity.

Your soul is what God had in mind when He first thought of you. He wasn't pondering your height, weight, dimension, ability to play an instrument, draw, sing, or shoot hoops. He was architecting your soul, your *imago Dei*, the image of God within you, giving you morality, rationality, and the capacity for relationship with Him.

He connected your soul to a unique physical existence, and now that soul blesses you with joy and love that starts somewhere deep inside you and shows up on your face and flows out through your hands. It challenges you with sorrow and anguish that lays you low. Somewhere in its domain is what tells you to say "no" to that third chocolate Ho Ho in the morning and what sets you on a course to hit the gym three times a week instead. It endows you with intelligence, wisdom, and wit and causes you to laugh at things others think aren't funny. It is who "you" are.

Lots of people seem to claim the quote, but someone said, "You don't have a soul. You are a soul. You have a body." That might be a stretch. Perhaps better said: We simply are not people—not humans—without our souls.

The soul is a central theme in the Bible.

---

5   John Ortberg, *Soul Keeping: Caring for the Most Important Part of You* (Grand Rapids, MI: Zondervan, 2014), 39.
6   Ortberg, *Soul Keeping*, 42.

In the Gospel of Mark, Jesus invites us in with words of freedom: "Come to me, all you who are weary and burdened, and I will give you rest" (Matthew 11:28).

This invitation has always been at the heart of faith in Jesus—a call for our souls to rest, to trust, to connect with the One who created us. And yet, how often do we pay any attention to that inner call or allow ourselves the space and permission to step away from life's disorder and let Jesus shepherd our souls?

When our bodies are neglected, we can experience a host of repercussions: unhealthy weight gain, an increase in heart disease, high blood pressure, and chronic illness. A weakened immune system can develop. We might lose sleep or have muscle and joint pain, cardiovascular or digestive problems, fatigue, and low energy.

Am I depressing you?

When we neglect our souls, we lose connection to our very purpose. We are separated from relationship with the God who made us, and we drift from alignment with the will of God. Distance from our Creator is widened. The fruit of the Spirit (Galatians 5:22, 23) is diminished, and worry, fear, and unrest rush in to fill the vacancy. Temptation becomes more difficult to resist, and the enemy of our soul gains strategic life footholds.

In the Old Testament, the Hebrew word *nephesh* is often translated "soul." This term appears more than 750 times and carries a range of meanings: life, self, being.

In Genesis 2, we read, *"The Lord God formed the man of dust from the ground and breathed into his nostrils the breath of life, and the man became a living creature* [nephesh]*"* (v. 7, ESV, author addition). Not just a being with a head, torso, legs, arms, and pulsing arteries and veins, but someone with a life-giving essence as a gift from God.

In the New Testament, the Greek word *psyche* is used to describe the soul. In Matthew 16, Jesus teaches: *"For what is a man profited, if he shall gain the whole world, and lose his own soul* [psyche]*?"* (v.26, KJV, author addition)

It is the part of you that connects with God, the One who created you, who is Spirit. It is how we know we are created in His image. God is not body. You look nothing like Him in that way. He is not a green-eyed, blonde-haired guy with a 32" waist and bulging biceps—or in my case, a slightly graying, blue-eyed, 34" waist, yet satisfactorily handsome man.

He is Spirit. You also have a spirit that connects with God—but your soul is the essence of who you are.

Your inner person via your soul is how you know you don't have four legs or dig holes in the ground to live in. It distinguishes you, not only as a created human but as a spiritual being—the genius creation of all God's work. You have a past, a present, and a future. You're thinking about that future right now. You aren't canine. Dogs aren't thinking about the future—not about tomorrow or even about thirty minutes from now. They only want to get their tummies rubbed and treats fed to them this minute. They live in the moment. They aren't waiting anxiously for the next turn of events. They live for now.

You don't. You live for your long-term dreams, hopes, and desires. That's your soul talking.

The soul is a seat of emotion—David, the psalmist shows us. *"Why, my soul, are you downcast?. . . . Put your hope in God"* (Psalm 42:11).

Job echoes it: "Have I not wept for those in trouble? Has not my soul grieved for the poor?" (Job 30:25)

Mary sings it. *"My soul glorifies the Lord and my spirit rejoices in God my Savior"* (Luke 1:46-47). She uses her soul to glorify God and then uses her spirit to celebrate what God has done to save her. Glorifying God is human behavior and responsibility. We express our humanity to God through our souls and magnify His power and presence through our souls.[7]

|||||||||||||||||||||||||||||||||||||||||||||||||||||||||||||||||||||||||||||||||||||

Soul care is not a luxury meant to be satisfied on the occasional vacation—it's daily fuel.

|||||||||||||||||||||||||||||||||||||||||||||||||||||||||||||||||||||||||||||||||||||

The soul has an eternal nature. Jacob's wife, Rachel, gave her newborn son his name "as her soul was departing" (Genesis 35:18, ASV).

---

7   Glory Dy, "What Is the Difference Between a Soul and a Spirit?", *Christianity.com,* 16 Dec. 2024, https://www.christianity.com/wiki/salvation/difference-between-a-soul-and-a-spirit.html#google_vignette.

Matthew 10 reinforces the forever condition of the soul: "Do not be afraid of those who kill the body but cannot kill the soul. Rather, be afraid of the One who can destroy both soul and body in hell" (Matthew 10:28).

Before we go any further, you might be saying to yourself, *I agree it's a great idea to press pause to care for my soul—to take a break. I just can't find the time. My life is busy. My schedule is crowded. My family demanding. My job consuming.*

I get it. I understand.

Let me encourage you. Soul care is not a luxury meant to be satisfied on the occasional vacation—it's daily fuel. You can't afford not to. Pressing pause when you know you don't have time for it is a grand acknowledgement that God is in control of it all, not you.

If you don't make time for it, your body and mind will eventually force you to. Taking a pause—even a short one—to care for yourself, bears good fruit. It makes you more loving, more self-aware, more productive in the long run, less prone to burn out physically, mentally, relationally, spiritually. It's like driving a car without ever stopping for gas. Eventually, you will run out of steam—you will break down.

That's why caring for our souls is more than just a good idea; it's a mandate modeled by Jesus Himself.

» He got to quiet places to be alone with His Father, talking, listening, praying. Jesus went up on a mountain to pray after multiplying loaves in Mark 6, and He withdrew to the wilderness after being inundated by the crowds in Luke 5.

» He practiced Sabbath rest.
» In Mark 2:27, Jesus reminded his followers that "The Sabbath was made for man, not man for the Sabbath," reinforcing the importance of slowing, not striving.
» He set boundaries.
» Jesus knew when and how to say no and when to step away. He made time for what mattered most and showed that loving others doesn't mean exhausting ourselves.

Luke 5:16 tells us Jesus paused often. Often. This wasn't an act of "Me first" or evasion of others; it was an act of necessity. He had to. Needed to.

Think about it. The Son of God needed to pause in order to care for His soul.

How much more should we?

PAUSE HACK: Enjoy your morning drink in silence. Savor your coffee or tea without distractions. No scrolling—just be present.

Chapter 2

Rebel With a Pause

"When the soul is well, the rest will follow."
—Anonymous

I don't know that I'm a soul rebel at heart, but I know what it feels like to be tired in places sleep can't reach. I know the ache of being constantly available, constantly expected to produce, constantly comparing myself to others. I know how easy it is to lose yourself while trying to keep up. And I know how brave it is to hit the pause button even for a moment—and how good that feels . . . after the guilt washes away, that is.

So maybe I'm not a rebel in the traditional sense. But I've learned that slowing down is a kind of protest. That turning off the noise is a kind of revolution. And every time I choose the pause over the output, I become a rebel (of the best sort).

These pauses impact us in personal ways, superficially and profoundly.

I have traded in my computer for a new one multiple times since I graduated from communicating via "chisel and rock" to something more sophisticated. It seems like every two to three years, I'm asking HR at our church for a new one. Even though I'm the pastor, sometimes they'll tell me it isn't my turn to be upgraded.

"Wait. You realize who I AM, right?"

"It doesn't matter. You still have to wait your turn."

"It doesn't M-A-T-T-E-R !?"

There are legit reasons I need a new one. Sometimes, it's fallen out of my satchel onto the paved church parking lot and gotten dinged—my unclasped satchel, to be fair.

At other times, there's been a key—or three—that, for some reason, sticks so that I'm forced to intentionally press those keys a little harder than the others, which throws off my typing rhythm and hinders me from being the productive person I'm called to be. I might also occasionally like to eat Cheetos with my fingers in between computer projects, but I digress.

I noticed that over time, certain keyboard symbols had become rubbed off so that all you could see was a weird, roundish glow coming from under those keys rather than the symbols themselves lighting up. I can type without looking, so it isn't a big problem, but it was a minor mystery to me.

When I got my newest Mac—after HR finally broke down—I decided I really wanted to keep this computer in good working order. I made a covenant with myself to treat it with extra care—satchel clasped, no more eating Cheetos out of the bag at my desk, a keyboard cleaner and air duster at my side. I'll show HR.

Because I was trying to take extra precautions and pay more attention to my Mac habits, I noticed within the first few days that my fingers tended to not just hover over certain keys, but actually rest on them. Not only that, I seemed to subconsciously massage those particular keys with my OCD fingertips when I paused to think—a perplexing practice and probably not something you want to include in a book. I came to the conclusion that, over time, the natural oils coming from my fingers must be rubbing out the symbols. Mystery solved, but I caught myself doing it over and over with those same keys until the very thought of me showing any kind of abnormal affection to my computer in this way drove me to stop.

What was interesting—and random—was that several of the keys my fingers arbitrarily slid to during these mental pauses were punctuation keys: the exclamation point, the period, the colon/semicolon—all keys that communicate grammatical pauses.

Evidently, syntax is my love language.

Just as musical rests are the heroes of symphonic pause, these symbols are the heart and soul of pauses when it comes to articulation. Without them you and I would rant nonstop like a caffeinated squirrel and nobody would know when to breathe or when a sentence ended or if we were asking a question or making a statement and honestly it would be absolute and ridiculous chaos like crazy-town I promise you it would be there's no doubt about it whatsoever so...

Ummm. See what I mean?

Harold Pinter was a twentieth-century British playwright and director—a Nobel Prize winner. He is credited with inventing what is now known as "The Pinter Pause." Pinter believed that theater did not accurately depict normal discourse or the complexities of language. For instance, when we search for words, we often pause—we think about what we should say next. Sometimes we say nothing at all in return—silence. This is how Pinter constructed his plays—with pauses and silences. It became such an effective hallmark of Pinter's plays that they named a pause after him.[8]

These are the kinds of pauses we utilize hundreds of times a day, and yet they are subliminal. At the other end of the spectrum are pauses that have the capacity to impact us for generations—cultural pauses that, in a solitary moment, have altered the world around us.

In 1962, at the height of the Cold War, the United States and then Soviet Union waged a stand-off over Cuba. The two countries entered a thirteen-day pause, negotiating to resolve the conflict. The short season was arguably one of the closest moments history has had to nuclear war, but it

---

8   Nicholas Ephram Ryan Daniels, "What are Pinter Pauses? And other Pinteresque devices," *London Theatre Direct,* last updated 18 Feb. 2021, https://www.londontheatredirect.com/news/what-are-pinter-pauses-and-other-pinteresque-devices.

was the pause that allowed cooler heads to prevail and for the world to be saved.

Martin Luther King Jr.'s "I Have a Dream" speech was given at the March for Jobs and Freedom in Washington, D.C., in 1963. King's skillful use of pauses throughout gave his words exponential power and resonance. They captivated his audience and made his vision unforgettable, even to this day.

That same year, President John F. Kennedy was assassinated. America watched as popular newscaster Walter Cronkite announced his passing on live television. His emotional presentation was punctuated with silent pauses as his audience was riveted by the shocking news.

The nation stood in collective grief and solidarity when more than three thousand lives were lost in the terrorist attacks of 9/11. Every year since, on that day, people pay their respects with moments of silent pause.

Pauses, whether peripheral or paramount, have a purpose. God has used waiting periods from the beginning of time to teach us, prepare us, encourage us, comfort us, warn us, and strengthen us.

God's Pause Before Creation

"In the beginning God created the heavens and the earth. Now the earth was formless and empty, darkness was over the surface of the deep, and the Spirit of God was hovering over the waters" (Genesis 1:1-2). The entire story of the Bible begins with an aura of stillness as the Spirit of God poises and pauses over the waters. Before any words by anyone are

spoken, the pause captures the beauty, mystery, wonder, and power of creation. It is a divine pause before the coming explosion of light and life.

Job's Pause

"Then they sat on the ground with him for seven days and seven nights. No one said a word to him, because they saw how great his suffering was" (Job 2:13).

Job's friends respond to his immense suffering with a heart-wrenching silence for seven days. Think of sitting with a grieving friend for 150-plus hours, saying nothing at all.

Could you do it? Would you?

This striking long-term pause underscores the inadequacy of words and the wonder of sharing the simple gift of humanity with someone else.

Elijah's Encounter with God

The LORD said, "Go out and stand on the mountain in the presence of the LORD, for the LORD is about to pass by." Then a great and powerful wind tore the mountains apart and shattered the rocks before the LORD, but the LORD was not in the wind. After the wind there was an earthquake, but the LORD was not in the earthquake. After the earthquake came a fire, but the LORD was not in the fire. And after the fire came a gentle whisper. —1 Kings 19:11-12

Elijah's rendezvous with God on Mount Horeb is one of the most profound moments in the Bible. One of Israel's great prophets has just won a spectacular victory over the prophets of Ba'al on Mount Carmel. He calls down fire from heaven to prove God's power, and the people ultimately turn against the worship of the false god.

In the aftermath, Queen Jezebel threatens Elijah's life as he flees into the wilderness. He's despairing, fearful, isolated, hopeless. Sitting under a broom tree, he begs to die: *"'I have had enough, LORD,'" he said. 'Take my life; I am no better than my ancestors'"* (1 Kings 19:4).

God responds not with rebuke but with compassion. He sends an angel to provide food and water, and Elijah gains strength to journey forty days and nights to Mount Horeb, also known as Mount Sinai—the place where Moses encountered God hundreds of years before.

At Mount Horeb, Elijah takes shelter in a cave. Here, God asks a question: "What are you doing here, Elijah?"

Elijah pours out his heart, lamenting the unfaithfulness of the people. Then God tells him to stand on the mountain because He is about to pass by.

What follows is one of the most iconic sequences in Scripture:

» A mighty wind tears through the mountains. But the Lord was not in the wind.

» An earthquake shakes the ground violently. But the Lord was not in the earthquake.

» A fire consumes the mountain. But the Lord was not in the fire.

Then a gentle whisper—a still, small voice. Don't speak—or you'll miss Him as He passes. Just listen. It is in this quiet moment—this holy pause—that Elijah senses the presence of Elohim.

Elijah might have expected a display of God's power, like what happened at Mount Carmel with the false prophets. But God reveals Himself unexpectedly...subtly...personably...intimately...with a whisper.

You must pause in order to hear it.

This gentle response by God invites you and me to quiet our hearts, slow down, and listen—to pause amid the clutter of life and learn that silence and "pauses" can be holy, because it is in these moments we encounter God most emphatically.

Jesus's Pause with the Adulterous Woman

"Jesus bent down and started to write on the ground with his finger. When they kept on questioning him, he straightened up and said to them, 'Let any one of you who is without sin be the first to throw a stone at her'" (John 8:6-7).

When the Pharisees challenge Jesus to condemn this woman, He doesn't respond right away. He implements a notorious pause by bending down and writing on the ground in the sand. This creates a tension unlike any other in Scripture—a pause that the accusers respond to by coming face-to-face with their own hypocrisy, dropping their stones, oldest to youngest, and walking away.

The Pause During Jesus's Trial

"The chief priests accused him of many things. So again Pilate asked him, 'Aren't you going to answer? See how many things they are accusing you of.' But Jesus still made no reply, and Pilate was amazed" (Mark 15:3-5).

Jesus's answer to His accusers during His trial is a weighty silence. It demonstrates His humility and submission to God's will, but also His resolve to walk the path of sorrow that ultimately leads to forever joy. He confounds those who expect a defense with a holy pause that changes the course of the story and history.

The Pause at the Crucifixion

It was now about noon, and darkness came over the whole land until three in the afternoon, for the sun stopped shining. And the curtain of the temple was torn in two. Jesus called out with a loud voice, "Father, into your hands I commit my spirit." When he had said this, he breathed his last. —Luke 23:44-46

At the moment Jesus's victory is completed, the earth joins in a pause of darkness and soundlessness. The universe mourns the death of the Savior—creation groans. The pregnant pause introduces humanity to the redemptive plan of God that continues still today.

The Three-Day Pause in the Tomb

Between Jesus's crucifixion and resurrection, there is an eerie silence that fills the narrative. For the disciples, these few days must have felt like an eternity of uncertainty. This pause heard around the galaxy is a prequel to the power and exhilaration of Easter morning.

The Pause at the Lord's Table

"So then, whoever eats the bread or drinks the cup of the Lord in an unworthy manner will be guilty of sinning against the body and blood of the Lord. Everyone ought to examine themselves before they eat of the bread and drink from the cup" (1 Corinthians 11:27-28).

Just before eating the bread and drinking the cup, we're each told to observe a spiritual pause. First, examine your heart. As Psalm 139:24 says, *"See if there is any offensive way in me."* What needs to be sacrificed, submitted, forgiven, and brought to the table of grace before receiving what is so graciously offered for you?

Upper Room Pause

Before receiving the Holy Spirit at Pentecost, the disciples are told to wait in Jerusalem for the Spirit to come. This pause prepared them for the power they would receive to witness for Jesus (Acts 1:4).

Heaven's Pause

"When he opened the seventh seal, there was silence in heaven for about half an hour" (Revelation 8:1).

This Biblical hold-your-breath pause heightens the anticipation of the return of Jesus—a cosmic pause, filled with awe, anticipation, and for some, foreboding.

Throughout, pauses are signposts that something is about to happen. There is wonder on the other side of the pause. These moments are not the absence of communication—they are a form of it. God speaks in the pause.

The Psalmist's Pause

The book of Psalms is a songbook and a prayer book. The term Selah occurs seventy-one times in thirty-nine of the Psalms, often repeated within a psalm. For example, Psalm 3:2-4 (ESV) describes a trust in God in times of trouble, reflecting on his faithfulness:

Many are saying of my soul,
"There is no salvation for him in God."
Selah.
But you, O LORD, are a shield about me,
my glory, and the lifter of my head.
I cried aloud to the LORD,
and he answered me from his holy hill.
Selah.

Psalm 46:10-11 (ESV) speaks of God's sovereignty, reflecting on His power:

Be still, and know that I am God.
I will be exalted among the nations,
I will be exalted in the earth!
The LORD of hosts is with us;

the God of Jacob is our fortress.
Selah."

Psalm 32:7 (ESV) tells of the protection of God, reflecting on His deliverance:
You are my hiding place;
You preserve me from trouble;
you surround me with shouts of deliverance.
Selah.

Although there is some lack of clarity around the term, many scholars view Selah as a musical pause in the text.[9]

It seems to have been understood by those who were playing and singing these psalms, if not also by those who were joining in singing. It is a form of musical punctuation and annotation, much like a rest in modern day music. This Selah pause could have been a request for the reader, listener or musician himself to pause and think about what has just been said or sung.[10]

Pond-Like Selah Moments

Imagine a still pond early in the morning. The water is calm like glass, reflecting the sky and trees above. You notice a small pebble on the ground, pick it up, and toss it in. The pebble hits the surface, creating ripples that spread

---

9   Ashley Lyon, "What Does *Selah* Mean?", *Logos,* 24 Jan. 2023, https://www.logos.com/grow/bsm-what-does-selah-mean/.
10   Jason Soroski, "What Does *Selah* Mean in the Bible and Why Is It Important?", *Crosswalk,*
13 Nov. 2024, https://www.crosswalk.com/faith/bible-study/what-does-selah-mean.html?gad_
source=1&gbraid=0AAAAAD4hHd8zpBWDwCJWb5-j_WcnJvdjv&gclid=Cj0KCQiA8q—BhDiARIsAP9tKI0eLq-T6ey
E72oT1cLZijmHm5zTrtrFk0VDWUoeC4BBoLqhIN-DlRMaAjrsEALw_wcB.

outward, breaking the stillness. For just a moment, everything changes—the reflection wobbles, the water stirs, and the sound of the pebble comes echoing back to you.

Now, imagine what happens if you keep throwing pebbles in one after another. The ripples collide and overlap, the water begins to churn, the peaceful reflections of a moment ago disappear. The constant motion wipes away the stillness.

But if you toss one pebble and wait, you can watch the ripples extend until they fade, the water returning to calm. In that moment of waiting, clarity and serenity are restored.

Selah is the pausing of the water. It is the "ah"—that moment after a long day when you breathe out a deep, peaceful, healing, "glad I'm home" sigh—where your shoulders drop a little, your chest softens, and the world feels a little lighter.

"Ah." Selah.

It's the moment when you stop tossing pebbles—stop striving, stop rushing, stop fretting—and let the tranquil ripples of life settle around you. It's the intentional break that allows you to reflect more deeply and hear God's voice more clearly amid life's volume.

Our hearts require still, pond-like Selah moments. Moments that reflect the beauty of God's existence, moments that absorb the impact of the storm. Without pauses, the ripples of constant busy thoughts and schedules drown out the peace God offers. But when we embrace Selah, we find renewal and connection with the One who created the stillness in the first place.

Selah. Meaning: Don't rush past. Enjoy the beauty of the moment. Rest in it. Pause to consider what God may be saying, even when you don't fully understand Him or His ways. Especially then.

Selah moments don't have to be complex. They are the sunrises and sunsets, the inhaling and exhaling, the space bars, rests, and punctuations:

» That first sip of coffee in the morning before the world wakes up.

» The serene shalom moment just after a prayer that we tend to rush past too quickly.

» The satisfying breath you take as you watch a rainbow span the sky.

These moments come and go far too quickly. We could sit in them longer. Selah reminds us that life isn't just about doing—it's also about receiving. It's releasing our burdens and allowing our souls to draw breath.

Psalm 61:4 says, *"I take refuge in the shelter of your wings."* Selah. Shalom. Stop for a moment. Pause. Repose. Reflect. "Ah."

A Parable of Selah

In the bustling city of Jerusalem, young Abel was known for his busy, restless nature. He was a scribe's apprentice, tasked with copying sacred texts onto parchment. The work was precise, requiring his greatest concentration, and Abel often struggled. His imagination wandered, his mind raced faster than his hand, and his impatience often led to mistakes. One day, while copying the Psalms, he encountered a particular word again and again—a word he didn't recognize or understand: Selah.

"What does it mean?" he asked his rabbi. "Why is it scattered throughout the text? Should I skip it or copy it down?"

The old rabbi chuckled, his weathered hands gently rolling a scroll. "Ah, Selah. It is not a word to rush past, my boy. Selah is an invitation."

"An invitation? To what?" Abel's brow furrowed in confusion and wonder.

"An invitation to pause," the rabbi said. "To stop, breathe, and reflect. Without Selah, the Psalms would be like water poured too quickly—it would be spilled, and its meaning would be lost."

Abel tilted his head in curiosity, "But isn't it better to keep going, to finish what we start? Why pause?"

The old rabbi beckoned him outside, where the sun was now beginning to dip behind the hills. The marketplace was still alive with activity—merchants bartering, children laughing, donkeys braying. It was chaotic by any measure. "Close your eyes," the rabbi instructed.

Abel obeyed without hesitation. As his eyes shut and the noise began to fade, he became aware of something he had neither seen nor heard with his eyes wide open—the rustling of leaves in the olive trees, the distant chirping of birds, the faint blowing of the wind. For the first time that day, he noticed the world had a rhythm that was always present, yet seldom observed.

"Do you hear it?" the rabbi asked.

Abel opened his eyes. "Do you mean the silence?"

"Not silence—the spaces between the sounds," the rabbi said. "That is Selah. In our lives, we must pause to hear what truly matters. Without Selah, we miss the voice of our Creator."

The next day, as Abel returned to transcribing, he approached each Selah with fresh care. When he reached the word this time, he stopped his quill, closed his eyes, and let the words he had just written sink into his heart. Slowly, he began to understand the Psalms not just as songs but as invitations to experience God's presence.

Years later, when Abel became a scribe in his own right, he passed the lesson of Selah to his apprentices. "Selah is more than a word," he would tell them. "It is the pause that allows us to hear the music of heaven."

IIIIIIIIIIIIIIIIIIIIIIIIIIIIIIIIIIIIIIIIIIIIIIIIIIIIIIIIIIIIIIIIIIIIIII

A Prayer to Pause

Dear Lord,
In the busyness of life, I come to You to press pause. I lay
aside my worries, my to-do list, and my distractions, to
be still and wait in Your presence. Help me slow down, to
breathe deeply, and to rest in the peace only You can give.
Quiet my mind so I can hear Your voice. Settle my heart
so I can feel Your love. Remind me that my worth is not
in my productivity but in being Your beloved child. Teach
me to embrace the sacred rhythms of rest, knowing that
You are at work even when it doesn't seem You are.

May this moment of pause renew my soul, refocus my heart, and draw me closer to You. Let me walk with fresh strength, guided by Your wisdom and filled with Your peace. Amen.

IIIIIIIIIIIIIIIIIIIIIIIIIIIIIIIIIIIIIIIIIIIIIIIIIIIIIIIIIIIIIIIIIIIIIIIII

PAUSE HACK: Put on headphones without playing music. People will assume you're busy and will leave you to yourself.

IIIIIIIIIIIIIIIIIIIIIIIIIIIIIIIIIIIIIIIIIIIIIIIIIIIIIIIIIIIIIIIIIIIIIIIII

Now... let's begin.

As each chapter concludes, there is an opportunity for you to engage in personal soul care. Don't let these moments pass you by. They matter. Not every reader may have a full hour to dedicate each time. These practices are meant to draw you into deeper soul care, but if time is short, don't feel pressured to do it all at once. Let the Holy Spirit set the pace. You might spread a single practice over a couple of days or simply pause for ten to fifteen minutes with the part that speaks to you most in that moment. The goal isn't to complete an hour—it's to be present with Jesus.

Having private time with God is essential for deepening your relationship with Him, and spending one hour with God makes a difference.

It helps you push back and rebel against the harried pace of life ...

It stills the fast lane of life and sets you in His presence...
Helps you gain clarity and peace...
Reminds you that He's ever present and that His plans for you are good...
Allows you to release burdens and cares and confess sins...
Leads you to spiritual renewal and healing...
Fills you with all the fruit of the Spirit...
Builds your faith...
Equips you to face the day with a fresh perspective...

This is where pausing to care for your soul becomes more than words on a page; it becomes life and a way of life. Enjoy this journey.

||||||||||||||||||||||||||||||||||||||||||||||||||||||||||||||||||||||||||||||

1-Hour Soul Pause Application: Psalm 46

It's okay if you're unable to complete the entire practice in one sitting. Give yourself permission to move at a pace that's gentle and sustainable—soul care isn't a race, but a journey of presence and grace.

To embrace the beauty and import of soul care, find a quiet and private place where you can be fully present with Jesus.

Things to have with you:
» A Bible (paper or digital)
» Something to write with
» Earbuds
» Your phone

You are encouraged to write in your book. By dedicating this hour to soul care, you align your heart with God's peace and presence.

Minutes 1-10: Center Yourself in Stillness
First, take some deep breaths. Focus on the presence of God. Don't rush this moment. Practice *being* with God.

Read Psalm 46 two times. Read slowly. Let each verse sink into your soul. If you finish early, sit in the stillness and learn to enjoy God.

Minutes 10-20: Meditate on the Protection of God
"God is our refuge and strength, an ever-present help in trouble" (Psalm 46:1).

How have you experienced the faithful protection of God in your life? Take time to journal those thoughts below.

(**Notes about journaling:** Journaling is a powerful form of communication with God. It is simply recording what is happening in your spiritual life. Since we have a tendency to forget the things God has done or fail to realize what He is doing right now, journaling is an antidote to forgetting/not realizing. Journaling helps us become aware of our spiritual progress. It is not a diary. It is a record of your relationship with God, what you are experiencing, learning, believing.)

_____

_____

_____

_____

_____

_____

_____

_____

_____

Minutes 20-30: Release Anxiety and Fear

"Therefore we will not fear, though the earth give way and the mountains fall into the heart of the sea" (Psalm 46:2).

What are the things your soul wrestles with—things that worry you—keep you up at night—make you at times wonder where God is in it all? Write them below:

The Wrestle:

_____

_____

_____

_____

_____

Scripture:

_____

_____

_____

_____

_____

Replace each anxious thought with a scripture that combats that thought. (Feel free to Google scriptures that address each worry.) Write that scripture on the second line above.

Now, pray through each worry or wrestle, praying the scripture you've written.

Minutes 30-45: Draw from the River of Peace

"There is a river whose streams make glad the city of God, the holy place where the Most High dwells" (Psalm 46:4).

Pull up a worship song on your phone—one that brings peace to your soul. If your private space has been invaded by now, use your earbuds. If possible, take a walk as you "press play."

Listen . . . and worship. Let your soul be refreshed by the presence of God.

Minutes 45-55: Declare God's Power

"The LORD Almighty is with us; the God of Jacob is our fortress. Come and see what the LORD has done" (Psalm 46:7-8).

Continue walking—or find a place to sit.

Speak words of faith to yourself.

Declare the power of God in your life.

Express how God has brought security and peace to you and your family.

Minutes 55-60: Be Still

"Be still, and know that I am God" (Psalm 46:10).

Just sit in the presence of God without saying anything—listen for His voice.

In these final five minutes, what is God saying? In just one or two sentences, what do you hear? Don't make it complicated. What is the first thing you sense? Write that sentence below.

_____

_____

_____

Ask God to help you carry His presence throughout your next twenty-four hours.

"Beloved, I pray that all may go well with you and that you may be in good health, as it goes well with your soul."
—3 John 2 (ESV)

||||||||||||||||||||||||||||||||||||||||||||||||||||||||||||||||||||||

"After silence, that which comes nearest to expressing the inexpressible is music."
—Aldous Huxley[11]

Each chapter from here forward includes a music track that expresses the heart of that chapter. The track is a spontaneous piano piece created and performed by the author and includes a classic hymn. Enjoy.

---

11 Aldous Huxley, *Music at Night and Other Essays* (London, England: Chatto & Windus, 1931), 19.

Song:

"IT IS WELL WITH MY SOUL"
by Horatio G. Spafford (1873)[12]

---

12 Horatio G. Spafford, "It Is Well with My Soul," 1873, Public Domain.

Chapter 3

Still Waters, Wild Grace

"The shepherd doesn't love the sheep because they are worthy; He loves them because they are His."
—Attributed to Max Lucado

The sun was just beginning to dip below the horizon, painting the hills of Judea in golden hues as the shepherd leaned on his staff, surveying his flock. It had been a long day of leading his sheep through rugged terrain, across rocky paths and rushing streams, but they had finally reached the greenish pasture where they would rest for the night. As he did every evening, the shepherd began his nightly count, his voice calm and steady as he called each one: "Daisy ... Ember ... Ruby ... Clover ... one, two, three, four . . ." To every other eye, they looked exactly alike, but not to him. He could tell by the way that one leaned a bit to the left when she walked. This one by an ear that had been tangled in a thorn bush a year ago until he was pried away by the shepherd. Another by the upturned grin that wasn't really a grin, just a malfunction at birth that made her look like she was always smiling. "Max . . . Tessa . . . Lilly . . . Wooly . . . Puff . . . Buttons . . . 94, 95, 96, 97, 98, 99 . . ."

One by one, the sheep lifted their heads, recognizing his voice and their own name, so familiar were they. It wasn't just a roll call—each title carried meaning, reflecting memories of their unique personalities.

With the count complete, the shepherd's brow furrowed. One was missing. "Luna?" He called again, louder this time.

"Luna?"

Silence.

He walked some paces, looking left to right, right to left, to the crest line of the hill, and then scanning the meadow below. Nothing.

His heart sank. Luna was one of the smaller and more curious of the flock, and she tended to wander. Likely, she had spotted some tender patch of extra green too tempting not to taste. Or . . . she had spotted a butterfly and could not resist chasing it. Or . . . something worse. Wandering could be dangerous.

The shepherd didn't hesitate. He left the flock in the safety of the enclosure and set off to find her.

The one.

Night was falling quickly. He must hurry. He heard his own voice drifting back as an echo across the valley as he called her name again and again: "Luna! Luna! Luna!"

Then, his years of expert tracking paying off, he spotted a faint trail of hoof prints leading down a ravine. Not a safe place for a sheep to wander.

He made his way down, and as the light was fast fading, he saw her caught in a thicket, her young and soft fleece entangled in brambles, bleating softly.

"Luna!" the shepherd cried with relief. Kneeling beside her, tears of joy streaming down his face, he carefully freed her and brought her close. His gentle voice a medicine, he nuzzled her against his chest. She nuzzled back, recognizing not only the sound of his voice, but the touch of his hands and the security they represented.

Carrying her on his shoulder, the shepherd made the arduous climb back to the flock. He spoke to her softly the whole way, reassuring her with words she didn't fully understand but whose tone said it all. As they approached the enclosure, the other sheep gave bleats of "Welcome home."

He settled Luna back with the rest of the flock and sat down among them, whispering each of their names once more and reassuring himself with a fresh count ... "95, 96, 97, 98, 99 ... Luna, 100."

Each one mattered. Each one belonged.

That night, under a blanket of stars, the flock rested peacefully, knowing their shepherd was near and watching over them. As for the shepherd, he stayed awake a little longer than normal, weary but content, his heart full of gratitude for his joy, his flock.

The Good Shepherd

As much as Jesus knows all things, has all power, is everywhere present, has no beginning and no end, is holy and just and eternal, it is His presence in our lives as our Shepherd that is perhaps our most compelling image in the context of soul care. The Twenty-Third Psalm is the classic "pause" text to help us understand who the Great Shepherd is and how cared for we are by Him. It cannot be read quickly. It must be absorbed with all the starts and stops intended when David wrote it.

|||||||||||||||||||||||||||||||||||||||||||||||||||||||||||||||||||||||||||||||||

The Shepherd gives us anything that is in alignment with his character and vision for our lives.

|||||||||||||||||||||||||||||||||||||||||||||||||||||||||||||||||||||||||||||||||

Pause to take it in. Set the book down for a second or two after each line and ponder what you just read:

The LORD is my shepherd, I lack nothing. (pause)
He makes me lie down in green pastures,
he leads me beside quiet waters,
he refreshes my soul. (pause)

He guides me along the right paths
for his name's sake. (pause)
Even though I walk
through the darkest valley
I will fear no evil,
for you are with me;
your rod and your staff,
they comfort me. (pause)
You prepare a table before me
in the presence of my enemies. (pause)
You anoint my head with oil;
my cup overflows. (pause)
Surely your goodness and love will follow m
all the days of my life.
and I will dwell in the house of the LORD
forever. (pause) —Psalm 23

The description of Jesus as our Shepherd assumes the presence of sheep.

Hi, how are ya? Baaaa!

The psalmist kicks off with an ironclad assurance: *"The Lord is my Shepherd, I won't lack anything"* (Psalm 23:1, author paraphrase). Anything we truly need, that is. Anything that would prevent us from drawing closer to Him, that is.

The Shepherd gives us anything that is in alignment with his character and vision for our lives. He will not abandon his sheep. He will not lead them with harshness or exploit them. He will not forget them or leave them behind. He never fails to provide and protect from the natural enemies of the sheep.

These "anythings" are the promises of a loving, faithful, sacrificial Shepherd.

But He does not promise every "anything"—and He calls His sheep to some "anythings" of their own. He calls them to give up anything that hinders their relationship with Him or prevents them from following His lead. He asks them to fully surrender, recognizing that apart from Him, they can do nothing. He calls them to turn from sin and any worldly desires. To let go of fear and worry, trusting in His provision rather than being anxious about life. To place their hope in eternal things rather than in earthly riches. To give up any and all bitterness and unforgiveness, just as the Shepherd has forgiven them. To abandon pride and the pursuit of status and embrace humility instead.

It is a more than fair trade, because He offers treasures of forgiveness, salvation, redemption, and eternal life. Through His sacrifice we are made new. Given a new start. New minds. New thoughts. New habits. New speech. New hearts. New motivations.

The Shepherd grants us peace that defies understanding and ensures that we are never alone. He becomes our healer, our sustainer, our provider. Even in seasons of less-than, He demonstrates that He can be trusted. He is our comforter when we are weary, our ever-present companion who never leaves us. Whatever challenges we face, He reminds us that because of Him we have the grace and strength to overcome.

No matter the circumstances, we have Him. We never lack. He is more than enough. He gives us His presence, and that is everything.

The psalmist goes on to say: *"He makes me lie down"* (Psalm 23:2). In other words, he makes me pause.

We have three daughters. They're grown now but when they were small there was something common to all three. They hated naps. I'd welcome a nap anytime, including right now, but she could be sitting in a chair nodding off, eyelids heavy as iron, and if I asked, "Honey, are you tired?" her answer would predictably be, "No, Daddy, I'm not tired"—though she could barely finish the sentence.

Even as I carried her upstairs to her room, her head bobbing at every step, she would still strain against my arm, insisting she didn't need to lie down. But I knew she did. And I would hang around quietly in her bedroom, sometimes sitting in the corner chair in the dark to ensure she stayed in bed. I was more determined that she lay down than she was determined to get up.

Philip Keller, in his work A Shepherd Looks at Psalm 23, writes that sheep do not lie down easily and will not unless four conditions are met. Because they are timid, they will not lie down if they are afraid. Because they are social animals, they will not lie down if there is friction among the sheep. If flies or parasites trouble them, they will not lie down. Finally, if sheep are anxious about food or hungry, they will not lie down. Rest only comes because the shepherd has dealt with fear, friction, flies, and famine.[13]

Here's what that looks like for us, and this is powerful.

Sheep, like us, can scatter at the slightest sense of danger. But having the shepherd nearby reassures us in the middle of uncertainty. The most common exhortation in the Bible is "fear not"—365 times—one for every day. The shepherd brings that well-being deep into the camp.

Every follower of Christ experiences friction—it is one of the lesser-welcome fruits of relationships. The Shepherd maintains harmony and unity in the flock via His presence. He guides us by His own example in resolving conflicts both great and small with love and humility.

Irritations are part of life. The Shepherd even takes time to deal with the annoying "flies" that buzz about us. He applies oil to our heads in the form of godly wisdom and self-control that protect His sheep, safeguarding us from intrusions and bringing the kind of promised peace that surpasses logic.

And famine? We need the Shepherd to find the pastures that are healthy and nutritious for our souls and bodies. Left to themselves, sheep can easily wander into barrenness. The Shepherd finds the lushest green to feed from. We depend on Him—physically, emotionally, relationally, spiritually—for provision.

These help us lie down and experience the pause He desires for us.

---

13 W. Phillip Keller, *A Shepherd Looks at Psalm 23: Discovering God's Love for You* (Grand Rapids, MI: Zondervan, 2007).

"He leads me beside quiet waters, he refreshes my soul, he guides me in paths of righteousness for His name's sake."
—Psalm 23:2-3

He leads. He refreshes. He guides. Three verbs, one after the other. Three ways the Shepherd cares for us. Three reasons to pause and fully embrace Him.

The Good Shepherd Leads Us

Since sheep aren't the brightest animals in the pen (do you remember I said you and I are sheep?), they need to be shown the way forward...pointed in the right direction. A good shepherd doesn't just give commands but walks alongside, showing the sheep where to go and how to get there.

> *For the shepherd, the sheep aren't just animals—they are his responsibility and pride. When the grass fields are thinning, the shepherd understands that his flock needs fulfilling nourishment. He whistles softly, and the sheep lift their heads. They trust him. He begins to walk through the herd gently, touching some while nudging others with his staff. He leads them over rocky terrain and through narrow paths, finally arriving at lush pastures. The hungry sheep graze there and are satisfied. The shepherd ensures that the sheep find what they need, even when they don't recognize the need themselves.*

We often find ourselves in situations where we think we know best, and yet we don't fully grasp what we need. Our souls become restless. Lost, even. There have been times when things didn't go as planned, only to later realize that by following the Good Shepherd, the outcome was far better than it would have been otherwise—a reminder that God's plan is always greater than ours.

Joseph, the favorite son of Jacob, had dreams that predicted his future greatness. But things took an unexpected turn. Several unexpected turns.

» He receives a special coat from his father, and his brothers become jealous.

» His brothers sell him as a slave into Egypt.

» He's falsely accused of attacking an official's wife.

» He's thrown in jail.

» He interprets an inmate's dream while in prison, and when the time comes, nobody remembers that he did.

» He ends up in front of the Pharaoh with the pressure of interpreting his dreams, or else.

» One of his predictions is of a terrible, impending seven-year famine—not a soothing message for the Pharaoh.

» Egypt is devastated by the famine. Joseph's own family, too.

In the middle of it all, because of his devotion to God, Joseph is promoted to second in the kingdom, in charge of the very food recovery that would save the nation, including his brothers and their families, so that Joseph could say at the end: *"You intended to harm me, but God intended it for good to accomplish what is now being done, the saving of many lives"* (Genesis 50:20).

It wasn't the plan anyone could have foreseen. But every trial and hardship has a God purpose. God gets good results from circumstances that, on the surface, seem not so good.

"He brought his people out like a flock; he led them like sheep through the wilderness" (Psalm 78:52).

Your wilderness, your physical and spiritual testing ground, is the place you learn to depend on God, no matter how dry and hot the desert. Sometimes God allows doors to close, relationships to end, famines to rise, plans to change—not as punishment, but as redirection. Our vision is limited, but in His perfect knowledge, God protects us from camouflaged harm—some of which we never fully understand in our lifetime—but we know it steers us to something greater.

The good Shepherd leads us.

The Good Shepherd Refreshes Us

"He refreshes my soul" is a reminder that restoration is a work of HE— the divine—the Good Shepherd. Refreshing is about bringing energy and hope to the sheep. It is about creating moments of renewal that they desperately thirst for.

> *As the sun climbs higher in the sky and the day grows hot, the sheep begin to pant. The shepherd knows they need water, but sheep are skittish and won't drink from rushing streams. They seem to instinctively understand that should they fall in, the water would soak through their heavy woolen coats and they would drown. Leading them to a brook that is still, calm, and shaded guarantees*

they have a safe and satisfying place to drink. Some of the younger, more inexperienced lambs hesitate, unsure. The shepherd kneels down, cups his hand in the stream, and splashes a little on their faces. It gives them the gumption to step forward to drink their fill and enter into the security the shepherd knows they truly seek.

As human "sheep," the challenges of life can leave us drained. Life can sometimes feel relentless with constant demands pulling us in every direction. We need times that rejuvenate our spirit and give us hope. These moments aren't merely about pausing to take a nap before we drag ourselves back up; they're about pausing to gain soul refreshment so we can soar. *"They who wait for the LORD shall renew their strength; they shall mount up with wings like eagles; they shall run and not be weary; they shall walk and not faint"* (Isaiah 40:31, ESV).

||||||||||||||||||||||||||||||||||||||||||||||||||||||||||||||||||||||||||||||||||||

The Good Shepherd doesn't just want you unstuck; He wants you to be revitalized, so your soul can prosper.

||||||||||||||||||||||||||||||||||||||||||||||||||||||||||||||||||||||||||||||||||||

There are particular ways our spirits can be refreshed. Scripture itself brings guaranteed encouragement and renewal when we feel empty. *'The law of the LORD is perfect, refreshing the soul"* (Psalm 19:7).

The Spirit of God promises to revive us, supplying joy and power for every day: *"That times of refreshing may come from the Lord"* (Acts 3:19).

We cannot underestimate the power God gives each of us to bring uplift and belonging to others by speaking a kind word, praying for another, or reminding someone that better things are possible in Christ: *"Whoever refreshes others will be refreshed"* (Proverbs 11:25).

The Good Shepherd doesn't just want you unstuck; He wants you to be revitalized so your soul can prosper.

The Good Shepherd Guides Us

Guiding isn't the same as leading. Leading supplies direction. It beckons, "Follow me." Guidance is more personal—it's hands-on. Not only "Follow me," but "Let me help you find the way."

The Good Shepherd does both. He reminds us that we've made progress and that there's more progress to be had. He walks with us, supporting us, holding up a lamp to help us navigate life and overcome challenges, providing wisdom, and buoying us along the way.

Sherpa guides are invaluable to Everest explorers because of their critical knowledge of local terrain, weather, mountaineering techniques, their physical adaptations to high altitudes, and their understanding of safety and survival in a harsh environment like the Himalayas.

That journey up the high and at times dangerous mountain isn't about one individual; it's about the team. If the sherpa has no plan, there is little hope of survival. Every trip includes the unexpected, whether it's a blizzard, predators, obscured paths, or other obstacles. A good sherpa makes instant and wise adjustments for the safety of the group. His role isn't to lead from a distance. He climbs and endures the mountain's surprises alongside the team. As a result, trust is built.[14]

> *As the sun begins to set, the shepherd gathers the flock to lead them back to the safety of the pen. On the way, a faint howl echoes in the distance. The sheep bristle. Their ears twitch. They sense danger close by. The shepherd-guide doesn't panic. He steps between the flock and the direction of the sound, holding his staff firmly and watching intently. His voice is calm—nothing more than a "coo" really—he knows his sheep. It's enough to settle them. He helps them find their way while keeping a vigilant eye out for the enemy. The shepherd guides them to their destination. "You're safe now." They don't grasp the words, but they know. It's OK. They can rest.*

The path of righteousness that He guides us in is Himself. He *is* the pathway.

"*I will guide you along the best pathway for your life. I will advise you and watch over you*" (Psalm 32:8, NLT).

---

14 Frank Belen, "Leadership Lessons from a Sherpa," *SHIFT,* 5 May 2016, https://www.shiftthework.com/blog/leadership-lessons-from-a-sherpa.

"You make known to me the path of life; you will fill me with joy in your presence, with eternal pleasures at your right hand"(Psalm 16:11).

When we pause, space is created to trust the Shepherd's path rather than our own impulses. The pause makes us conscious that we don't have all the answers and that we actually need to be guided—we are desperate to be.

If we fail to pause, we risk straying, we become exhausted and miss the gentle directions of the Shepherd's staff.

The Good Shepherd can be trusted to guide us.

In the Valley, Too

"Even though I walk through the darkest valley, I will fear no evil, for you are with me; your rod and your staff, they comfort me. You prepare a table before me in the presence of my enemies. You anoint my head with oil; my cup overflows" (Psalm 23:4-5).

> *It's later than normal, and the shepherd has finally led the sheep from the valley back to the pen. With the delay to find the one that was lost, he has walked with his staff higher than normal so they can see where He is guiding. They have passed through the dark howls of the night and made it home. Now, under the full blanket of security, the shepherd does one final check. He's always counting—many times a day, he is. One seems to be limping now. He kneels. Something is embedded in her hoof. A nasty thorn. The shepherd works to remove it. Carefully. The sheep flinches, but his touch is gentle, yet thorough. His voice firm but soothing. Once the thorn is*

> out, the shepherd cleans the wound and applies oil so
> it can heal. He carries the sheep to a separate corner to
> rest, away from the flock, ensuring it won't be distracted
> or cause further strain to the one. As darkness falls, the
> shepherd sleeps at the entrance to the pen, becoming
> the door to protect his flock. Any predator will have to
> go through him first. The sheep sleep soundly, knowing
> they aren't alone, assured by his presence.

Beautiful, providential promises like this are echoed throughout Scripture:

"*I will never leave you nor forsake you*" (Hebrews 13:5, ESV).

"*I am the good shepherd. The good shepherd lays down his life for the sheep*" (John 10:11, ESV).

"*He tends his flock like a shepherd: He gathers the lambs in his arms and carries them close to his heart; he gently leads those that have young*" (Isaiah 40:11).

Ironically, Jesus is not only the Good Shepherd; He is the "Lamb of all," as graphically described in the Old Testament:

> *Surely he took our pain*
> *and bore our suffering,*
> *yet we considered him punished by God,*
> *stricken by him, and afflicted.*
> *But he was pierced for our transgressions,*
> *he was crushed for our iniquities;*
> *the punishment that brought us peace was on him,*
> *and by his wounds we are healed. . . .*
> *He was oppressed and afflicted,*
> *yet he did not open his mouth;*

he was led like a lamb to the slaughter,
and as a sheep before its shearers is silent,
so he did not open his mouth. —Isaiah 53:4-5, 7

The Lamb became the Shepherd, and the Shepherd became a Lamb, and now He calls us to gentle pauses as an act of divine care.

Rest.

Have no lack.

Lie down.

Walk by still waters.

Experience the wildness of My grace.

Let your soul be refreshed.

Know My guiding presence.

Fear no evil.

You are not alone.

Be comforted.

Sit at My table.

Let Me fill your cup.

Sense My goodness, mercy, and love.

Know the safety of My house.

Louie Giglio says it so beautifully:

> *When you allow Jesus to be your Shepherd, He steps into this stressed-out culture and becomes your replenishing guide. He leads you, watches over you, and gives you rest. Jesus gives you purpose. He shows you how to deal with your enemies so they don't tear you apart inside. Jesus*

> *gives you hope and a future, and He'll restore your soul.*
> *He'll give you goodness and love for today, for tomorrow,*
> *and for every day for the rest of your life.*[15]

If you live very long at all, you'll find that life holds uncertainties, challenges, and crossroads. Without direction, it's easy to lose your way. The Good Shepherd illuminates the path and provides the clarity needed to navigate the complexities life presents.

Because we are the rebel lost sheep who have been found, soul care begins by understanding who your Good Shepherd truly is.

IIIIIIIIIIIIIIIIIIIIIIIIIIIIIIIIIIIIIIIIIIIIIIIIIIIIIIIIIIIIIIIIIIIIIII

A Prayer to the Shepherd

Dear Jesus, my Good Shepherd,
I come before You as a sheep in need of Your care. You
give me everything I need. I am satisfied in You. You
know my heart, my struggles, and my wandering ways.
Thank You that You never stop guiding, protecting,
comforting, and calling me back to Your side. Thank
You for leading me beside still waters, for restoring my
soul, and for walking with me through every valley.
When I am lost, find me. When I am weary, carry
me. When I am afraid, remind me that You are
near. Teach me to trust Your voice, to follow where
You lead, and to bask in the safety of Your love.

---

15 Louie Giglio, *Don't Give the Enemy a Seat at Your Table* (Nashville, TN: Thomas Nelson, 2021), 23.

*Shepherd my heart, Lord. Keep me close, and let
me never stray from Your presence. I surrender to
Your care, knowing that in You, I lack nothing.
Amen.*

IIIIIIIIIIIIIIIIIIIIIIIIIIIIIIIIIIIIIIIIIIIIIIIIIIIIIIIIIIIIIIIIIIIIII

PAUSE HACK: While drinking morning coffee, tea, or juice, take a moment to pause in between sips and actually enjoy it, instead of mindlessly gulping it down and getting on your way.

IIIIIIIIIIIIIIIIIIIIIIIIIIIIIIIIIIIIIIIIIIIIIIIIIIIIIIIIIIIIIIIIIIIIII

1-Hour Soul Pause Application: The Good Shepherd

It's okay if you're unable to complete the entire practice in one sitting. Give yourself permission to move at a pace that's gentle and sustainable—soul care isn't a race, but a journey of presence and grace.

To embrace the beauty and import of soul care, find a quiet and private place where you can be fully present with Jesus.

Things to have with you:

» A Bible (paper or digital)
» Something to write with
» Your phone

You are encouraged to write in your book. By dedicating this hour to soul care, you align your heart with God's peace and presence.

Minutes 1-10: Self-Examination

You are the hardest person to lead. That's why the first step to engage in meaningful soul care is to examine your own heart and soul.

> *"Search me, O God, and know my heart: try me, and know my thoughts: And see if there be any wicked way in me, and lead me in the way everlasting"*
> —Psalm 139:23-24 (KJV)

Take a few minutes to really examine yourself. Ask:

____ Is there anything preventing me from being completely present with Jesus today?

____ Are there distractions that need to be dealt with— physical, mental, relational, heart distractions?

____ Is there personal sin that needs to be addressed?

____ Is there anyone you need to forgive or ask forgiveness from?

Confession Prayer

Minutes 10-25: Psalm 23

Read Psalm 23 two times.

How have the blessings of God been evident in your life during each life season?

Think: *How/when have you been cared for by God? How/ when have you found rest, life, peace, satisfaction?*

Write your discoveries in each section below.
As a child:

_____

_____

_____

As a teen:

_____

_____

_____

Age 20-29:

_____

_____

_____

Age 30-39:

_____

_____

_____

Age 40+:

_____

_____

_____

Let your soul celebrate the above—see how much God loves you and watches over you. Take a moment to be thankful.

Minutes 25-35: Right Paths
"He leads me in paths of righteousness for His name's sake."
—Psalm 23:3 (ESV)

That begs the question: HOW?

Eugene Peterson suggests that David, the author of Psalm 23, experienced at least three things that shaped his soul: David's PRAYING, MEDITATION, and ADORATION.[16]

Using that as a soul template, ask yourself:

» How could I better include PRAYER in my day-to-day life going forward?
» How could I better include MEDITATION in my day-to-day life going forward?
» How could I better include ADORATION in my day-to-day life going forward?

Take a moment to examine the above in your life.

Minutes 35-55: The Valleys
Read the 23rd Psalm again. Focus on verse 4: *"Even though I walk through the darkest valley, I will fear no evil, for you are with me."*

David certainly understood what it meant to walk through a valley. He knew the discomfort and pain of it, but he also grew to know the benefit.

What is your valley? Are you in one right now? More than one?

---

16 Eugene Peterson, "Meditating Like a Dog," *Christianity Today*, May 31, 2007 (excerpt from *Eat This Book*).

Take a moment to name it/them. A valley could be a person, a place, a thing, a situation or a circumstance. What is it?

_____

_____

_____

_____

_____

Jesus walked through valleys. Select two or three from the list below to look up. Let your soul be encouraged by the fact that Jesus navigated difficult seasons, too.

» Testing by Satan (Mark 1:12, 13)
» The storm at sea (Mark 4:35-40)
» Pushback from others (Mark 7:1-5)
» Personal desperation (Mark 14:32-36)
» Betrayal (Mark 14:43-46)
» A close friend denies Him (Mark 14:66-72)
» Ultimate humiliation (Mark 15)

As you read through your selections, put your own valley into perspective.

Lift up a prayer, however God is leading you in this moment.

Minutes 55-60: Finishing Up (ten minutes)
Spend these last moments in thanksgiving to God for all your soul has discovered in this hour. Pull up a favorite worship song on your phone as background.

"Beloved, I pray that all may go well with you and that you may be in good health, as it goes well with your soul."
—3 John 2 (ESV)

Song:

"Jesus Loves Me"
by Anna Bartlett Warner (1859)[17]

---

17 Anna Bartlett Warner, "Jesus Loves Me," 1859, public domain.

Chapter 4

Who's Your Doppelganger?

"To be yourself in a world that is constantly trying to make you something else is the greatest accomplishment."
—Attributed to Ralph Waldo Emerson

After attending that first silent prayer retreat, I began to unapologetically embrace the power of pausing to care for my own soul on a regular basis. I decided, as the leader of a young and growing church team, that it was my call to encourage them and help them honor these pauses in their own lives. The initial group that benefited from these times was our leadership team.

I spent time praying and poring over Scripture. Then, I created three-hour-long spiritual guides that they would each work through on given days. They were to utilize these guides by finding an isolated place from morning till lunch to pause to be with God. The only stipulation was that "pausing" at home or the office was off limits; both places were so familiar that thought (and child) distractions would be almost automatic. The conclusion of the soul-care time included connecting them in threes over lunch with team cohorts to download their experience with Jesus. It was a time of spiritual enrichment, God-connection, and relationship building among the team.

Soul-care days were scheduled four times a year. I could tell they anticipated and cherished these days of refreshing. Over time, other church teams followed us for our intentional pausing to care for the part of us most deeply connected to Jesus—our souls.

One day, right after the leadership team had finished their soul-care day and returned to the office for the remainder of the work hours, I happened to be walking along the back hallway of our church in the afternoon. The windowless passage was dark and cold. I remember it was winter. Wisconsin, where I live, really only has two seasons: "Winter is here" and "Winter is coming." This was "Winter is here."

Someone was approaching from the other end of the corridor. It bends in the middle, and I couldn't yet see who it was, but I could hear the swishing of his arms against his coat as he strode in my direction. As I rounded the bend, I saw it was someone from our production team. A good man who was doing incredible work for the Kingdom.

As he came upon me, he stopped.

"Today was soul-care day for the team, PK?" (That's what they call me.) It was not so much a question as a statement.

"Yes, it was."

He nodded an affirmation, but didn't walk on. His head was bowed a little lower than what seemed natural, eyes searching the carpet. There was no question put forward, but I answered as if there had been one: "It's important that they take time to care for their souls."

His response revealed an honest emotion and sentiment he had obviously been dealing with longer than that lone walk down the back hall. What he said flattened me against the wall, and I don't think I've been the same since.

"I have a soul, too."

I couldn't bring myself to speak. I just looked at him with a rising sense of guilt, shame, and conviction.

Yes. Yes, you do.

In that moment, before moving on, I laid my hand on his shoulder as a gesture of care, and my eyes met his as an affirmation that I had heard him. The lump in my throat prevented me from vocalizing anything meaningful.

I had neglected encouraging the rest of our team with an opportunity to soul pause—all people I was responsible for. I had put my focus on those who carried a particular title, not acknowledging something I knew full well—that souls are the one thing all humans have in common, and all souls need to be cared for in order to flourish as followers of Jesus.

Of course, we all have a soul, but he was saying something deeper—more significant and weighty: *Help our souls be healthy, Pastor. We get dry and thirsty too. We want to know more of Jesus.*

From that moment forward, every employee—full- or part-time—was invited to experience these soul pause moments together. Required to.

Souls matter. Yours does. Because you have a soul too.

Who Am I?

Pause for a moment to consider: Who am I . . . really? Why do I matter? What gives my life value?

Until we answer these questions, we won't come into right relationship with the One who created us.

Hiroshi Ishiguro, a professor at Osaka University in Japan, spent decades pushing the boundaries of human-like robotics. In the early 2000s, his work reached an unprecedented level. He set out to build an android that was a nearly perfect replica of himself.

Using silicone skin, precise actuators and advanced AI, Ishiguro and his team crafted what he called Geminoid HI-1, a robotic doppelganger. The android mimicked Ishiguro's facial expressions, gestures and mannerisms. He even had the android attend conferences and lectures in his place while he controlled it remotely, watching through its cameras and speaking through its speakers.

As the project advanced, something strange happened. Ishiguro began to question what it really meant to be human.

But rather than asking, "How close to human can a machine actually become?" he began to ask, "Am I really just a machine myself? Did someone create me? How do I know for sure? What is reality and what isn't? Since I have created a duplicate so precise to the 'original'—(and am I truly an original?)—what then is the difference between human and artificial life? And is there a point where artificial actually becomes a form of human? Can that bridge be crossed?"[18]

For some, Ishiguro's work blurred the lines between creator and creation. Alarmingly so. Geminoid HI-1 was separate from him and yet able to interact with the world in his place as his reflection, able to *be* him in ways even he had not anticipated.

The question that hung in the air was: Have I built a machine? Or have I, in some way, built another version of myself?

In His Image

If you take a life-size piece of paper and a sharpie and draw on it the best representation of a human you can draw—something that looks so life-like and detailed and then hold it up next to you and ask: "Which of us is the creator and which is the created?"— you would universally get the right answer: *You* are the creator. *It* is the created.

You, as the creator, know better.

You, as the creator, are wiser.

You, as the creator, can bring the creation's existence to an end.

The same is true if you carved the most incredible sculpture of yourself—or molded one with human dimensions

18 Ericco Guizo, "A Japanese roboticist is building androids to understand humans—starting with himself," *Deraffe*, https://deraffe.io/2021/02/16/hiroshi-ishiguro-the-man-who-made-a-copy-of-himself/.

from clay—or painted one—or built a robot that was, to all but the most discerning eye, the spitting image of you—you still created it. You did. You're the creator. That thing is the created. It might have texture. It might have a body. It might have inner workings. It might be able to touch, speak, hear, see, move, respond. It might, someday, even have human-like organs sustaining it—but it does not have a soul. It is an "it."

||||||||||||||||||||||||||||||||||||||||||||||||||||||||||||||||||||||||||||||||

Not only did God knit and create your soul, He knitted it in His image.

||||||||||||||||||||||||||||||||||||||||||||||||||||||||||||||||||||||||||||||||

The soul is what makes us human, not our bodies. You do not have the capacity to create a soul. A likeness, yes. A machine, yes. Perhaps even some kind of body. But not a soul. That is beyond your pay grade.

God made your soul.

For you created my inmost being;
you knit me together in my mother's womb.
I praise you because I am fearfully and wonderfully made;
your works are wonderful,
I know that full well.
My frame was not hidden from you

when I was made in the secret place,
when I was woven together in the depths of the
earth. —*Psalm 139:13-15*

God stands by waiting for us to pause for a moment to acknowledge and worship Him as the sole Soul Knitter. I don't know a whole lot about knitting—"knit one, purl two" is about the extent of my knowledge—and frankly, I'm not that interested in learning more, but I know it takes a plan and a design for the piece to come to life. Not only did God knit and create your soul, He knitted it in His image. *Imago Dei.* Image of God. Think of it. You're made like Him, with intrinsic worth and dignity.

Remarkable and beautiful. Delicate, yet strong. Courageous, but sensitive.

I know someone with a tattoo on the back side of his upper arm that says "IMAGO DEI." It might be the most profound thing I've seen indelibly imprinted on a person's body. It gets my vote for the thing to brand your skin with forever, if you're going to do that kind of thing.

The concept of being made in the image of God is one of the most transformative concepts in Scripture. It is the picture we see of God—the image.

We pay close attention to that image because it is related to how we see ourselves. Juanita Ryan says:

> *It has been my observation that for every distortion*
> *a person has of God there is usually a corresponding*
> *self-distortion. If we see God as a vengeful, punishing*

> *God, we are likely to see ourselves as bad and as deserving*
> *of punishment. If we see God as a person with impossible*
> *expectations, then we will likely see ourselves as a failure*
> *or as not good enough.*[19]

That image shapes who we are. It is the foundation for any soul work we pause to do. It answers those most fundamental questions asked earlier: Who am I? And why do I matter?

Answer: You are a child of God. You matter because He chose to create you, to will and speak you into existence.

They say no two snowflakes are exactly alike. I don't know who's taken the time to research all that, but I've heard enough people say it that I'm bought in. There are actually snowflake photographers—people who take pics of frozen snowflakes laid on black fabric before they can melt. One such gentleman, Wilson Alwyn Bentley from Vermont—which sounds like a great place to capture snow-flakes—took five thousand pics and insisted no one flake was like another.

Humans share that quality. Dr. Roger J. Williams, a bio-chemist at the University of Texas, said it well: "All of us are basically and inevitably individuals in many important and striking ways. Our individuality is as inescapable as our humanity. If we are to plan for people, we must plan for indi-viduals, because that's the only kind of people there are."[20]

19 Juanita R. Ryan, "Seeing God in New Ways: Recovery from Distorted Images of God," *The National Association for Christian Recovery,* https://www.nacr.org/center-for-spirituality-and-recovery/recovery-from-distorted-images-of-god-seeing-god-in-new-ways-recovery-from-distorted-images-of-god.
20 Lawrence Reed, "Humans Are Snowflakes," *Frontier Institute,* 26 Mar. 2024, https://frontierinstitute.org/humans-are-snowflakes/.

No one in history has ever been exactly like you—nor will there be another. Your thoughts, experiences, and giftings are one of a kind. As the French are fond of saying, *"Vive la différence!"* You have God and God alone to thank for that.

So, why do you matter? You matter because your worth isn't earned by you, and yet it is deeply rooted in you, inseparable from who you are. Your existence has meaning and purpose, even if you haven't fully figured it out yet. You were positioned at this time and place for a reason. Your presence makes a difference.

Imago Close to Home

Our daughters are all adults. They look alike in many ways and yet are unique. They are miracles of wonder and individuality as well as evidence of the creativity of a God who creates billions of people and not one of them is a carbon copy of the other—not even twins.

Some think our daughters look like me; others believe they resemble their mother. They have inherited features from each of us—the beauty, eyes, skin tone, and hair color of their mother—the nose and big feet of their father.

Here and there, you see people who remind you of someone else, though unrelated. Their mannerisms seem similar. Their features are almost identical, though not exact. You've been at a restaurant and thought for sure you spotted someone on the other side who you knew. You approached to say "hi," only to find that once you got within feet of them, it was only someone who looked like them.

And then you had to think of an excuse to get out of why you had already slapped them on the back.

I've been told I look like several famous people. I use the word "famous" broadly, but we all have doppelgangers out there in the big world. I'm told some of mine are Joe Namath (if you're under forty-five, Google him), Dick Van Dyke (same), a weatherman on the local news (I can see this similarity), Jeff Goldblum, and when people are being extra nice to me and I imagine need to schedule a visit to the eye doctor, Jeremy Allen White and Hugh Jackman. None of these people looks anything like the other, but for some reason, I look like each of them in some way. Go figure.

I look like my father. He passed away on Veterans Day, 2020, at age ninety. We weren't close, and I knew next to nothing about him or his life. In fact, we had only seen one another perhaps five times in my adult life, but the "imago" between us was striking. At his funeral, several people mentioned that of his seven children (all of them half-siblings to me), I looked most like him. Again, go figure.

The *imago* goes deeper. He had four different wives, the last one he married in retirement. They visited me one afternoon—the last time I saw him before he died—travelling from their home in Kansas City to where I live in Wisconsin. His wife noticed the floor-to-ceiling, wall-to-wall shelves in my office where I have displayed 1:18 scale model cars from the '40s, '50s and '60s. It's a hobby and collection I've enjoyed and added to for years. If I can't have a garage of full-sized vintage cars—my dream—I can at least have scaled-down versions to admire (and play with when nobody's looking). She pointed out that my father had a lot of these very same cars displayed on shelves at their home.

Surreal.

She proceeded to tell me about a couple of habits he had that, according to her, were quirky. Every night before bed, he had to have two Oreos and a glass of milk.

What!? Whenever my wife allows Oreos in the house, I'm eating them every night with whole milk. I am the King of Quirk that way.

She told me his favorite dessert was a thick chocolate milkshake.

Well! Everyone who knows me understands that I am a chocolate milkshake aficionado.

Imago Dei. In the image of. The Imago surpasses what you look like. You actually don't look like God, physically speaking. It is a picture of his nature, His values, and purpose that you carry.

The phrase "made in the image of God" appears first in the Genesis creation narrative.

> *Then God said, "Let us make mankind in our image, in our likeness, so that they may rule over the fish in the sea and the birds in the sky, over the livestock and all the wild animals and over all the creatures that move along the ground."*
> *So God created mankind in his own image, in the image of God he created them.*
> *—Genesis 1:26-27*

This proclamation sets humanity apart from all other creatures. Unlike plants and animals, humans are not only crafted with intentionality—they are created with the greatest potential and an unquestionable need for intimacy, reflecting something important about their Creator. In His image.

The Hebrew word for "image" (*tselem*) refers to a representation, while "likeness" (*demut*) emphasizes similarity or resemblance. Put together, these terms signify that humans are a reflection of God in a way no other part of His creation can claim. Both man and woman are created in His image and likeness.

The Genesis account shows that the act of God breathing life into Adam proves that human existence flows from a divine source. *"Then the LORD God formed the man out of the dust of the ground and breathed into his nostrils the breath of life, and the man became a living being"* (Genesis 2:7).

Job 33:4 echoes this: *"The Spirit of God has made me; and the breath of the Almighty gives me life."*

Unlike Rover the dog or Garfield the cat or Punxsutawney Phil, we have God-breathed souls. Imago Dei does not suggest we can look in a mirror and see His physical likeness. Imago Dei describes attributes that reflect God's character and work in us. We have the ability and calling to exercise dominion and authority over creation—expressions of our souls that work their way out through our hands and feet.

But that divine image became stained by sin at the fall of humanity. That fall distorted the Imago, but it did not erase it. Enter Jesus, the Redeemer.

He is the radiance of the glory of God and the exact imprint of His nature" (Hebrews 1:3, ESV).

Through Jesus, "the image of the invisible God" (Colossians 1:15), the Imago is beautifully and miraculously re-made in believers through redemption, salvation, and transformation by His Spirit (2 Corinthians 3:18).

In essence, God . . . sent God. The God of creation who threw the stars into space and at the command of His voice set the galaxies spinning is also the One who sent His one and only Son to leave the glory and splendor of a perfect heaven to humbly put on skin and walk among us—to show us the way—to give His life under the most brutal circumstances so we could experience life and love and be with Him forever. God sent God.

||||||||||||||||||||||||||||||||||||||||||||||||||||||||||||||||||||||||||||||||||||||||||||||||

Imago Dei helps us understand we are not accidents—we are created with direction, intentionality, and meaning.

||||||||||||||||||||||||||||||||||||||||||||||||||||||||||||||||||||||||||||||||||||||||||||||||

It goes further.

That we are made *imago Dei* means violence, racism, poverty, trafficking, injustice, assaults on the family, and the ill treatment of the unborn are affronts to the divine image placed inside each of us from before we were a seed in our mother's womb.

That's why nobody has to tell you certain things are right or wrong. We all bear the same imprint—one that has its source in the divine. You just know it. It flows from the inner part of you. No law has to be written to convince you. No "Ten Commandments on How to Treat Others" needs to be taped to your refrigerator. These things elicit a disturbance in the soul made by God, the *imago* inside us. They incite us to pause to comprehend who we and others really are in Christ.

Imago Dei helps us understand we are not accidents—we are created with direction, intentionality, and meaning. This gives life deep significance and shapes our calling to live in a way that honors our Creator. And while this *imago* at times becomes scarred, it can also be beautifully and miraculously restored.

"In [Jesus] we have redemption through his blood, the for-giveness of sins, in accordance with the riches of God's grace" (Ephesians 1:7, author addition).

No one is beyond that grace; everyone is welcomed into that grace, every person has the potential for grace-filled renewal, and each one is called to be a grace-giver. This is living out the *imago* that has been placed in us.

|||||||||||||||||||||||||||||||||||||||||||||||||||||||||||||||||||||||||

Years ago, a family called my office at the church I serve. They were not attenders and had never been to the church

WHO'S YOUR DOPPELGANGER? 105

before. They said they were looking for someone to offi-
ciate their son's funeral and passing our church building
every day on the main street in our city, they didn't know
where else to go.

"Would you do the funeral service for our son?"

Knowing nothing about them, I still consented. Funerals
are opportunities to do ministry that impacts eternity.
Having to choose between a funeral and a wedding, a
funeral might be my choice. Weddings are fun; funerals
can be life-changing for those still living.

We made an appointment for an in-person meeting.
When the father, mother, and sister of the deceased arrived,
our conversation led me to discover they were atheists. The
whole lot of them, including the deceased.

Privately, I was scratching my head why they would
be seeking help with a funeral in a church setting from
an evangelical pastor who believes in the reality of God,
heaven, and hell. During the course of our time together,
they asked a question that will forever be embedded in my
soul: "Pastor, can you tell us that our son is in heaven?"

Long, long pause by me.

Heaven? Meaning, the place with clouds where fat Cupids
play harps? And hell, where the guy in the red body suit
with horns and a pitchfork lives?

I shared the gospel with the three of them, and though
they did not receive Jesus in that moment that I know of,
that interaction was incontrovertible confirmation that the
imprint of God, the *imago*, lives in every person—and deep
down, we know it. I looked into a casket that day at a young

man's lifeless body, as did every member of his family—a body that had carried the *imago* Dei. God placed eternity in his heart (Ecclesiastes 3:11).

When it matters most, we cannot deny it.

Parable of the Golden Coins

In a great and prosperous kingdom, a Potter crafted a set of golden coins. Each coin was stamped with the royal seal, marking it as the king's property. The Potter made every coin with great care, ensuring that each one reflected the king's image in its design.

The king sent the coins out all over the kingdom, telling the people, "These coins bear my image. They have great value. Use them well, for they represent the worth I have placed on you."

At first, the people treasured the coins, treating them with honor and respect. Over time, though, some coins were lost, some dropped in the dirt, others became scratched and worn, and a few were traded as if they were worth little. Some people forgot the royal seal was imprinted on them and began to believe only the shiniest, newest coins had any value.

One day, the king's son travelled to the villages, gathering the forgotten and tarnished coins. He held each one up and spoke, "Though you are worn and covered in mud, your value has never changed. The image of the king is still on you."

The son carefully cleaned each coin, restoring its luster, and reminded the people, "You were made with purpose, stamped with the mark of the king. Never forget your worth."

From that day on, those who listened to the son treated every coin—whether old or new, scratched or smooth, soiled or clean—with great honor, knowing that its value had never changed and never would.

Being made *imago Dei* means we are created to reflect God's character, glory, and goodness. This truth naturally calls us to pause—not simply to acknowledge that He exists, but to openly praise Him—because recognizing our divine design inevitably leads us to worship our Creator. It is for His pleasure we were created (Revelation 4:11). That now becomes our primary purpose—glorifying Him. And we cannot fulfill that purpose without pressing pause. This is not a begrudging pause; it is a full-blown, arms outstretched, head up, smile on our face pause—an opportunity to remember why we exist at all—to exalt the One in whose image we are made.

||||||||||||||||||||||||||||||||||||||||||||||||||||||||||||||||||

A Prayer of *Imago Dei*

Heavenly Father,
Thank You for creating me in Your image. You formed
me with love and dignity, reflecting Your beauty in my
life. Help me see myself as You see me—not through the
lens of the world, but through the truth of Your Word.

*Teach me to honor Your image in myself and in others.
Help me treat every person with the grace and respect
You intended, knowing that each one of us displays
a picture of You and tells a story of You with our
lives. So help me live in a way that glorifies You.
Restore what is broken, renew my heart, and help me walk in
the fullness of who You created me to be. May I love as You
love, serve as You serve, and shine Your light in the world.
Amen.*

||||||||||||||||||||||||||||||||||||||||||||||||||||||||||||||||

PAUSE HACK: Put your phone in airplane mode today—or for a few strategic hours—no texts, no notifications, just uninterrupted peace.

||||||||||||||||||||||||||||||||||||||||||||||||||||||||||||||||

1-Hour Soul Pause Application: *Imago Dei*

It's okay if you're unable to complete the entire practice in one sitting. Give yourself permission to move at a pace that's gentle and sustainable—soul care isn't a race, but a journey of presence and grace.

To embrace the beauty and import of soul care, find a quiet and private place where you can be fully present with Jesus.

Things to have with you:

» A Bible (paper or digital)
» Paper to write on
» Pen to write with

» Your phone

You are encouraged to write in your book. By dedicating this hour to soul care, you align your heart with God's peace and presence.

Minutes 1-10: Quiet Reflection

Begin slowly—with silence. Spend five minutes to pause and "get yourself ready" for today's soul care. Just SIT with Jesus. (Play a quiet worship song from your phone as you begin this time.)

As you listen, pray that God would open your heart to what He wants to do in you in this hour.

Minutes 10-30: Reflection

Soul care is not solely about sitting and listening. That's part of it, but it is also about letting the power and beauty of Scripture into our lives and searching it for God's plan and purposes.

Look up the following Scriptures:

» Genesis 1:26-27
» Psalm 139:13-14
» Ephesians 2:10

Pause and ask yourself: How does the truth of these scriptures impact how you view yourself (and others)? Take them one at a time. Do you struggle at all to see yourself as an image bearer of God?

Now... close your eyes and imagine how God has crafted you lovingly in His image.

Next ... take out your phone camera. Take a look at yourself. Really look. (Maybe make sure nobody is watching you do this.) This is the person God made in His image, someone with great value, worth, and dignity.

Below . . . list your unique giftings and abilities, things you're good at, and blessings lavished on you by God. This is a moment to "boast in the Lord" for His gracious gifts to you. Don't skimp. Let your soul soar in this moment. Be grateful and blessed.

_____

_____

_____

_____

_____

_____

_____

Gratitude plays a major role in all soul-care activities. Pray a prayer of thanksgiving to God for all of the above. Review them, take them individually, and express your gratitude for what God has done. This is health to your soul.

Minutes 30-45: Journaling
Based on the above, write a letter to God as a declaration and commitment of how you will embrace and live out your *Imago Dei*.

Minutes 45-55: Others-Centered

Move it out beyond you for the final part of today's soul care. Others bear the same imprint as you do—God's *imago*.

Think of the people in your close circle of influence—family, good friends, relatives, co-workers. Determine to speak life into them this week. Take one per day. Who will you affirm each day—in person, by text, or phone video? Purpose to breathe life into their souls.

Monday—_____

Tuesday—_____

Wednesday—_____

Thursday—_____

Friday—_____

Saturday—_____

Sunday—_____

Minutes 55-60: Re-reflect

End as you began. Sit in stillness, letting God remind you of who you are in Him. Pull up that song again and enjoy the presence of the God who loves you and created you in His image.

Purpose to read Genesis 1:26-27 each day this week, affirming and re-affirming that you are made beautifully, lovingly, and powerfully *IMAGO DEI*.

"Beloved, I pray that all may go well with you and that you may be in good health, as it goes well with your soul."
—3 John 2 (ESV)

Song:

"OH! TO BE LIKE THEE"
by Thomas O. Chisholm (1897)[21]

---

21 Thomas O. Chisolm, "Oh, To Be Like Thee," 1897, public domain.

Chapter 5

Lessons in Horticulture

"When you recover or discover something that nourishes your soul, care enough about yourself to make room for it in your life."
—Jean Shinoda[22]

One of our favorite drives is through the small Italian villages of Tuscany. The rolling hills from Cortona to Montalcino are the stuff of a storybook. The morning sun bathes these knolls in a golden light, casting long shadows over olive groves and cypress trees. The air carries

---

22 Jean Shinoda Bolen, "When you discover something that nourishes your soul, care enough about yourself to make room for it in your life," *Good News Network,* 23 Feb. 2019, https://www.goodnewsnetwork.org/jean-shinoda-bolen-quote-on-nourishing-your-soul/?utm_source=chatgpt.com.

the faintest aroma of ripe grapes hanging in heavy clusters on the vines.

This is wine country, vineyard after vineyard telling stories of long labor, diligence, and loving work by its vine keepers.

In these villages, cobblestoned streets are lined with enotecas and wind through medieval settings encircled by ancient stone walls with mythical-sounding names: Montepulciano, San Gimignano, Lucca, Monteriggione, Pienza, and many more.

On our first trip there, staying at a family-run *agriturismo* outside Viaggi, the innkeeper led us on a personalized tour through stone cellars with floor-to-ceiling wine racks loaded with Chianti, his hands a faint purple from handling years of harvests. Barrels of wine live here, aging for years until they are deemed mature enough to come out into the sunlight. He poured us a glass of his very best, its translucent ruby-red hue catching the light overhead. I took the most polite and smallest sip I could since I don't drink, but if I did, I imagine it would have defined the most perfect harmony of earth and elegance in a glass.

"Here the land tells us what to grow," he boasted in his Tuscan accent reminiscent of something out of *Life is Beautiful*,[23] as he motioned proudly to vines stretching to the horizon.

"It isn't just a wine; it's how we live." He seemed to have a hundred slogans at the ready. "It teaches us patience and it is our way of love."

---

23 Roberto Benigni, *Life Is Beautiful* (October 23, 1998; Los Angeles, CA: Miramax Films).

The way of love.

In the earliest days of Christianity, believers in Jesus were referred to as "followers of the Way." A way of living, not to mention loving, beyond merely believing a set of doctrines. Really following.

Just before Saul's conversion in Acts 9 we read:

> *Meanwhile, Saul was still breathing out murderous threats against the Lord's disciples. He went to the high priest and asked him for letters to the synagogues in Damascus, so that if he found any there who belonged to the Way, whether men or women, he might take them as prisoners to Jerusalem. —Acts 9:1-2*

The connection to the earliest Christians calling themselves "followers of the Way" was related to Jesus's claim that He was "the way and the truth and the life" (John 14:6). His followers were walking a path other than those around them—a way of sacrifice, surrender, and love.

Tertullian, a second-century Latin theologian, writes of the difference between early followers and the culture around them. In one of his works, *Apologeticus,* he describes those differences:

> *The meals are modest . . . at which even the poorest of their members can eat and be satisfied. The banquets begin and end with prayer. . . . They are not violent with each other or their enemies. They don't kill their children, even in the womb. They are honest and don't steal. . . .*

> *They use their possessions for the good of others. They*
> *are chaste and don't surrender themselves to lust. . . .*
> *They seek the good of the world in which they live. . . .*
> *Their piety is as much an inward reality as it is an out-*
> *ward act. . . . See how they love each other.*[24]

May it be so with us.

John 15 is part of what many call "Jesus's farewell discourse," where He prepares His disciples for His soon departure, teaching them what it means to live on in His eventual absence. He says to them: "I am the true vine, and my Father is the gardener" (John 15:1).

In this poetic statement, Jesus identifies Himself as "the Vine," contrasting Himself with Israel, often referred to as a vine in the Old Testament (e.g., Psalm 80:8-16; Isaiah 5:1-7).

God intended Israel to bear good fruit and be a model to the nations all around them, but they so often failed due to their on-again, off-again relationship with Him. Jesus, however, is the ultimate fulfillment and example of what Israel was meant to be: a source of fruitfulness and faithfulness. The Father is described as a vinedresser—a gardener—carefully tending to the branches to ensure maximum fruitfulness.

The Father cares for the branches, supports the branches, tends to the branches. But not only that. The Father also cuts away and prunes. The cutting away is permanent. Those branches cannot be reattached to the vine and live again.

---

24 Tertullian, *Apology*, trans. T. R. Glover, in *Tertullian: Apology. De Spectaculis*, Loeb Classical Library 250 (Cambridge, MA: Harvard University Press, 1931).

The pruning, however, makes it possible for the branches to bear even more fruit, sometimes through difficulty, challenge, trial, and discipline (e.g., Hebrews 12:10-11).

My wife is a master gardener. Not officially—she has no degree or certificate for it—I just think she is. Compared to me, she is. I can't keep plastic plants alive, but she has one of the greenest thumbs I've seen. Kelly green. I feel great empathy for people she asks to come to our home to care for her plants when we're going to be out of town for an extended period. And by an "extended period," I mean four hours or more.

We were away once for a three-month sabbatical, and I grew hives on behalf of the poor soul who said "yes" to this assignment.

She has scores of plants around the house, inside and outside. According to her playbook, each of them requires unique and individual care. Each has a personalized regimen to stay healthy. They practically have personalities, according to her. If I accidentally step on one, you'd think I had just unleashed a global catastrophe. If you aren't a plant person, the instructions you're expected to absorb before you've completed the detailed in-home training would be overwhelming. Even the most horticulturally experienced has to be on his or her toes.

When she's gone for two or three days to visit family, I am assigned to watch over the plants in her absence. This is terrifying. I follow her around the house the day before as she points to various leafy children and doles out customized instructions:

"This one needs to be watered every day without fail."

She points to the one sitting next to that one. "This one can be over-watered, so be careful with it."

"How do I know if it's over-watered?" I ask.

"You'll just know."

I won't.

"Just feel the soil. If it's dry, give it some water. If it's moist, leave it alone."

I feel them. They all feel the same to me.

"This one feels dry, so I guess I should water it?"

"Don't water that one. That one's supposed to be drier."

"But . . ."

We head outside.

"All the kids in pots need to be watched carefully. Are you writing this down? Don't water with a hose; you'll break the stems. Use the watering can. But don't water the cactus. And if it rains, don't water anything. Things that are evergreen won't need watered either way. Deciduous plants, water. Annuals, water. Perennials, don't bother."

What's a perennial? I don't dare speak this out loud; I just think it to myself.

"Leave the tall grasses in the large pots alone."

"I thought everything in a pot needed to be watered."

"They do, but not those."

So I water them all. A little. Not too much. Just enough that they aren't dead when she gets home. And I pray like I've never prayed before. It's amazing how much damage you can do to a plant in two days. I know. I've done it. And faced the wrath.

I've watched her prune the oak leaf hydrangea (she told me that's what it was called) outside our backyard bay window. They quickly grow big and strong and are beautiful during summer and fall in their bold hues of pinkish-white. Their stalks develop into mini-trunks that take a chainsaw to cut through. When she's done pruning, they are a shell of their former selves. They look sorry and pitiful. I feel like these plants must be crying in a way that only someone in flower heaven can hear and empathize with, but they are just pruned. Nothing more or less. Still, she is ruthless. She takes a large clipper and goes at it like Edward Scissorhands all around the yard, giving various flora a military buzz cut.

"Are you sure that's helping?"

She's explained the process so many times over the years that she no longer dignifies the question. I'm still 100 percent certain that this time, the severe treatment will be the death of them.

It never is. They all have a bright future. They re-emerge the following spring bigger, bolder, more beautiful than ever, bearing more fruit than the year before. She was right. This miracle of nature is astounding—and guaranteed.

"He cuts off every branch in me that bears no fruit, while every branch that does bear fruit he prunes so it will be even more fruitful" (John 15:2).

I will confess this isn't the best news of the day. I would prefer a UPS-delivered Harry & David basket to show fruitfulness, not this. Human pruning can, by definition, be uncomfortable, and yet it is essential for the health and growth of your soul and to live in alignment with the purposes of God.

||||||||||||||||||||||||||||||||||||||||||||||||||||||||||||||||||||||||||||||||||||

Trusting in God with a hand that may seem harsh in the moment, though it isn't, frees you to live a life rooted in God's purpose and joy.

||||||||||||||||||||||||||||||||||||||||||||||||||||||||||||||||||||||||||||||||||||

The Master Gardener removes things that drain you—unhealthy habits, misplaced priorities, unproductive distractions. Pruning allows new growth to flourish and leads you toward greater wholeness. It shapes your character to reflect more of Jesus. But it isn't pain-free. It might come in the form of challenges that reveal areas in your life that need refining: pride, envy, anger, greed, impatience, fear, materialism, worldly ambition—a basketful of bad fruit whose roots have the capacity to dive deep and fast into the heart of you and latch on. While it may feel painful at the time, the pruning process strengthens virtuous fruit like humility, perseverance, and generosity. Trusting in God with a hand that may seem harsh in the moment, though it isn't, frees you to live a life rooted in God's purpose and joy. And maybe, just maybe, you finally stop dreading the pruning the way you did before you came to understand what He was doing in your life.

Then Jesus says:

> *"Remain in me, as I also remain in you. No branch can bear fruit by itself; it must remain in the vine. Neither can you bear fruit unless you remain in me. I am the vine; you are the branches. If you remain in me and I in you, you will bear much fruit; apart from me you can do nothing. If you do not remain in me, you are like a branch that is thrown away and withers; such branches are picked up, thrown into the fire and burned. If you remain in me and my words remain in you, ask whatever you wish, and it will be done for you."* —John 15:4-7

We must remain. Abide.

But how?

Enter . . . the pause. We create space to be with Jesus—space to know Him. To hear Him. To stay connected to His life-giving presence. Remaining and abiding are not linked to your performance or your stick-to-it-iveness. We make it so complicated, but the Gospel of John is clear. Your remaining is linked to your willingness to pause—to simply be with Him.

Imagine you're spending the entire day with a good friend. The conversation is easy and flows naturally, not confined to any topic in particular. You chat over breakfast, share thoughts during a walk, and throughout the day, exchange moments of silence that would break a lesser friendship. From start to finish, the connection remains constant and unbroken. Simple and comfortable. Genuine and valuable.

This is what abiding and remaining with Jesus looks like—a continual conversation that weaves in and out through every part of your day, including beautiful pauses where few words are traded. It's what Paul was describing when he exhorted us to "pray without ceasing" (1 Thessalonians 5:17, ESV).

A. W. Tozer says, "The man who would truly know God must give time to Him. Abiding means staying long enough to be shaped by His presence."[25]

When we stay attached to the Vine, our thoughts, ways, and prayers more easily align with His will. Our words are shaped by His voice, and we hear that voice answer us in the ordinary day. That voice shapes our plans and our lives and our Tuesday nights and Friday afternoons and ultimately our destiny.

We become disciples who remain—disciples who abide.

He still isn't done. "As the Father has loved me, so have I loved you. Now remain in my love. If you keep my commands, you will remain in my love, just as I have kept my Father's commands and remain in his love" (John 15:9-10).

History—notably our own—proves that we struggle to be with Jesus. I think I know why. Yes, we live in a world of distractions—phones, media, goals to be achieved, work and family responsibilities, the list goes on—but there is also spiritual resistance at play. You have an enemy. He

---

25 A. W. Tozer, *God's Pursuit of Man: Tozer's Profound Prequel to The Pursuit of God* (Moody Publishers, 2015), 20.

lurks about like a predator scouting out prey. He knows that just being with Jesus for even a few minutes will be transformative. He knows that the fruit of spending time with Jesus will bring peace, joy, patience, goodness, kindness, faithfulness, self-control, freedom—things he despises and is afraid of. So he throws guilty distractions in our path to keep us separated from the God who not only created us, but who wants us and loves us deeply.

But we feel that we need to fix ourselves before we come to Him. We believe we haven't prayed enough, read enough Scripture, or been good enough to be near Him.

||||||||||||||||||||||||||||||||||||||||||||||||||||||||||||||||||||||||||||||||||||||||||

God's melody over us is not a dirge of disappointment or frustration—it's a song of love.

||||||||||||||||||||||||||||||||||||||||||||||||||||||||||||||||||||||||||||||||||||||||||

We're like Peter, who, after meeting Jesus for the first time, experienced the largest fish catch of his career—so many that both his boat and the boat of his friends began to sink. When Peter saw that ,he fell at the feet of Jesus and said: *"Remove yourself from me, Lord; I'm so sinful and guilty I shouldn't even be in the same space with you right now"* (Luke 5:8, author paraphrase).

That's you and me, minus the fish and the boats. But Jesus never asks us to clean ourselves up before coming to Him. He simply says, "Come, follow Me." But we delay, resistant to letting go of certain things in our lives that we may not be able to take with us on that journey—things we consider valuable, even when we know Jesus is calling us to something better. We hold back because we don't fully grasp how much He really loves us. If we understood the depth of delight He has in us, we would run to Him without hesitation.

"The LORD your God is with you. . . . He will take great delight in you . . . [and] will rejoice over you with singing" (Zephaniah 3:17, author addition).

Not only does He take delight; He sings.

We see Him as a distant judge—but He sings.

A vengeful and punishing bully—no, He sings.

We think we need the perfect prayer life, the right amount of Scripture reading, or a rightly structured quiet time, when in reality, Jesus simply wants us to sit with Him for a while, to pause long enough to give Him our hearts. But pause we must.

And He sings.

God's melody over us is not a dirge of disappointment or frustration—it's a song of love. It's a melody of amazing grace, reminding us that we are cherished, not because of whatever good things we may have done or plan to do, but because of who we are in Him, who He made us to be. It's a song of peace, telling us we are safe in His presence. It's a song of hope, reassuring us that no matter how broken or lost we feel, He can restore us and make everything new.

If you listen closely—through His Word, by His Spirit, in paused moments of serenity—you'll hear Him singing:

You are my child.

You are always loved.

I will never leave you.

You are mine.

It might seem awkward at first. We are not comfortable with pausing. Pausing must be cultivated. But the more we practice being with Him, the more natural it becomes and the greater the fruit and reward. And the beautiful thing is, the more we are with Him, the more we want to be with Him—to abide and remain. All He asks is that we pause and listen to Him sing.

Abiding Love

There is one more thing before Jesus leaves this short sermon on abiding. We will touch on it later in the book, but it can't be ignored here.

> *"I have told you this so that my joy may be in you and that your joy may be complete. My command is this: Love each other as I have loved you. Greater love has no one than this: to lay down one's life for one's friends. . . . This is my command: Love each other." —John 15:11-13, 17*

Love. Each. Other.

Father Damien was a thirty-three-year-old Catholic priest who served a leper colony on Molokai, Hawaii, in the late 19th century. At the time, leprosy was a terrifying and misunderstood illness. Those afflicted were often isolated and sent to live in private communities to prevent the disease from spreading. One such colony was established on the island of Molokai. Conditions there were dire, suffering was rampant, and the victims of leprosy felt demoralized.

Father Damien volunteered to visit this mission. He knew the risks. Everyone did. Leprosy was contagious, and living among the infected meant likely contracting the terrible disease at some point. But genuine compassion is stronger than fear. Damien's heart burned with a love that would not let him stay in the comfort of his cushy parish in Honolulu while these souls suffered.

Father Damien didn't minister from a distance—ministry from afar is no ministry at all. He prayed as the boat docked, "Lord, let me be Your hands and feet. Let them see You in me."

The colony was worse than he had imagined—rundown shacks falling apart, filth in the streets, hollow-eyed people too weak to stand. Children wandered aimlessly, their faces marked by infection, their futures stolen from them.

But the most heartbreaking thing was the hopelessness. No one looked him in the eye. They had stopped believing they mattered long ago.

"Who are you?" a man rasped, his voice brittle with suspicion.

"I am Damien," Father said softly. "I've come to live with you."

The man laughed. "Live with us? You won't last a month."

Damien smiled. "We'll see."

True to his word, he lived among them, not as a distant preacher but as a brother. They became friends. He built homes and churches and schools and hospitals. He created a sense of community in a place where fear and despondency was the order of the day.

He treated them as equals, bandaging wounds and tending to those too ill to care for themselves. He dug graves. It was hard to find a mirror in Molokai during this time. Lepers tended to hide in the shadows, ashamed of their appearance, but Father Damien showed them the kind of care that proved they were worthy of grace and dignity.

Damien preached the love of Jesus to those who doubted such a thing could be real. He reminded them they were not forgotten ... not abandoned ... not turned away ... in fact, they were deeply loved and valued by God.

One Sunday morning, Damien stood before the congregation he had planted. He began the way he started every week: "My dear brothers and sisters ..." But this time he paused. He looked at them smiling, yet with tears in his eyes, and said, "We lepers ..."

The words hung in the air until they became a reality. Damien had contracted leprosy. He was now one of them.

Father Damien continued to serve in Molokai for eleven years until his death in 1889 at the age of forty-nine. His life is a symbol of remaining out of love, abiding out of care, sacrificing for others, and embodying the grace-filled mercy of the One who loved us first.[26]

Love transformed Molokai in the late 1800s. In 2009, Father Damien was canonized as a saint in the Catholic Church. His story continues to inspire people of all faiths to serve others with a love greater than themselves.[27]

Pausing doesn't end with you. The fruit that remains gets shared.

There is a love that abiding in Christ reveals. Close your eyes and let the words wash over you: "Remain in Me." It is in no way a dictatorial command coated with guilt or pressure. It is an invitation, full of grace, peace, blessing and love.

Just when you think it's a two-way interchange, He moves it out in concentric circles, Father Damien-style: "Love others as I have loved you. Lay down your life for one another."

And there it is.

26 Denzil Walton, "Father Damien, His Life and Legacy," *Discovering Belgium,* 29 Oct. 2023, https://www.discoveringbelgium.com/father-damien/.
27 Donald Jacob Uitvulgt, "The Touch: On Saint Damien of Molokai and the love of Christ," *The Catholic World Report,* 10 May 2024, https://www.catholicworldreport.com/2024/05/10/the-touch/.

Pausing to care for your own soul leads outward. Beyond you. This is important. Pausing doesn't end with you. The fruit that remains gets shared. The Jesus model of love runs from the Father in heaven to Him—and then to us. But it doesn't stop there. It flows to those around us.

It is our central command—sacrificial love—shown to us by Jesus laying down His life and setting the standard for how we should walk as fruit of our remaining and abiding.

This is the resulting test of a soul that has discovered the treasure of Jesus the Vine.

So, we pause to remain. We get pruned. We bear fruit. We love one another.

Pause. Remain. Get pruned. Bear fruit. Love one another.
Pause. Remain. Get pruned. Bear fruit. Love one another.
Etc., etc., etc.
And your soul thrives.

||||||||||||||||||||||||||||||||||||||||||||||||||||||||||||||||||||||

A Prayer of Abiding

Lord,
I long to remain in You, to dwell in Your presence, to
draw my strength from You. You are the true Vine, and
I am a branch—without You, I can do nothing. Teach
me to stay connected to You in every moment, not just
in times of need but in the daily rhythms of life.
Help me to abide in Your love and rest in Your
goodness. When distractions pull me away, draw

me back. When life feels overwhelming, remind me
that You are my source of strength and renewal.
Fill me with You, that my life may bear fruit for Your glory.
Let my words, my actions, and my heart reflect You in
everything I do. May I find joy in walking closely with You.
Let me remain and abide in You today and always.
Amen.

||||||||||||||||||||||||||||||||||||||||||||||||||||||||||||||||||

PAUSE HACK: Set a fifteen-minute pause on your calendar sometime during the day. Use that time to sit in peace, ponder, sip a drink, or just space out for a while.

||||||||||||||||||||||||||||||||||||||||||||||||||||||||||||||||||

1-Hour Soul Pause Application: Abiding and Remaining

It's okay if you're unable to complete the entire practice in one sitting. Give yourself permission to move at a pace that's gentle and sustainable—soul care isn't a race, but a journey of presence and grace.

To embrace the beauty and import of soul care, find a quiet and private place where you can be fully present with Jesus.

Things to have with you:

» A Bible (paper or digital)
» Something to write with

You are encouraged to write in your book. By dedicating this hour to soul care, you align your heart with God's peace and presence.

Minutes 1-5: Start

Put yourself in a place to receive from Jesus today. Just quiet yourself and ask Him to come into this time you've set aside to be with Him.

Minutes 5-20: Quiet Reflection

Read John 15:1-11 two times.

REFLECT: What is your current relationship with Jesus, and how does this passage reflect that relationship?

Is there a place where your life doesn't fully reflect what you read here?

Write your observations below. Be truthful with yourself and with God.

_____

_____

_____

_____

_____

_____

_____

_____

Minutes 25-35: Pruning

Verse 2 speaks about "cutting off" and "pruning."

Have there been moments in your life when you have experienced pruning? When? How did those moments strengthen your soul so that it was more like Jesus? How did it lead to growth and create beauty and health in your life?

Write down any habits, attitudes, or distractions He may be asking you to release.

_____

_____

_____

_____

_____

Pray for courage and trust as you surrender these areas to God, knowing pruning is for your ultimate good and greater fruitfulness.

Minutes 35-55: Fruit

Read Galatians 5:22-23.

The first three fruits—LOVE, JOY, PEACE—are God's gifts to us.

The second three—PATIENCE, GOODNESS, KINDNESS—are how we interact with others.

The last three—FAITHFULNESS, GENTLENESS, SELF-CONTROL—describe what we become as the Holy Spirit transforms us.

Take them below one-by-one. What is the evidence of each in your life? Be encouraged as you write something that shows how the fruit have become part of who you are. Which fruit could have greater evidence in your life?

EVIDENCE OF THE FRUIT IN YOUR LIFE

LOVE _____

JOY _____

PEACE _____

PATIENCE _____

KINDNESS _____

GOODNESS _____

FAITHFULNESS _____

GENTLENESS _____

SELF-CONTROL _____

Ask God to develop each one in greater measure.

Minutes 55-60: Thankfulness

Be thankful for the fruit in your life. Each morning or evening this week, determine to spend time thanking God for these fruits.

"Beloved, I pray that all may go well with you and that you may be in good health, as it goes well with your soul."
—3 John 2 (ESV)

Song:

"AMAZING GRACE"
by John Newton (1725-1807)[28]

28 John Newton, "Amazing Grace," 1725-18025-, public domain.

Chapter 6

Wave a White Flag

"God cannot fill hands that are already full. Surrender what you're clinging to, and watch Him work."
—Anonymous

It began as an ordinary Sunday. The sun rose over the Pacific, casting its golden rays on the crystal waters and the quiet bustle of a naval base. Sailors shared coffee and breakfast aboard their ships, while others enjoyed a moment of leisure before the busy week resumed. Children played in nearby neighborhoods, and the Hawaiian air was filled with a sense of tranquility. No one could have imagined that in just moments, the peaceful calm would be shattered.

At 7:55 a.m., the roar of engines pierced the sky. Japanese aircraft, their red Rising Sun insignia visible even in the morning haze, descended on Pearl Harbor like a swarm of locusts. Bombers, fighters, and torpedo planes unleashed their fury on the unsuspecting naval base. Explosions thundered across the harbor as artillery struck the anchored ships, sending plumes of black smoke spiraling into the sky.

Naval crews scrambled in confusion and disbelief. Some thought it was a training drill—until the deafening blasts of dropped bombs and the sight of burning ships made the grim reality clear. The USS *Arizona* was struck by a massive projectile, igniting her forward ammunition magazine in a cataclysmic explosion. The ship's hull split in two as flames engulfed her decks with hundreds of men trapped below. The sound of their cries for help were muffled by the burgeoning chaos.[29]

Amid the destruction, acts of extraordinary heroism unfolded. Sailors dove into oil-slicked, flaming waters to rescue comrades. Medics worked to save the wounded. No one had time to process the horror—they were too busy fighting for their lives and for each other. Nearby the USS *West Virginia* listed and began to sink. Dorie Miller, a mess attendant having no training in gunnery, manned an anti-aircraft gun and shot down several enemy planes, just one of many who refused to give up. He was the first black recipient of the Navy Cross.[30]

---

29 James Laubler, "Pearl Harbor: The Waking of a Giant," *U.S. Department of Veterans Affairs*, 6 Dec. 2011, https://news.va.gov/5447/pearl-harbor-the-waking-of-a-giant/.
30 Tangie Woods, "First Black Recipient of Navy Cross & Medal of Honor Nominee: Doris 'Dorie' Miller," *Mrs. T's Corner*, 29 Aug. 2024, https://tangietwoods.blog/2024/08/29/doris-miller-first-black-recipient-of-navy-cross-medal-of-honor-nominee/.

As the first wave of attackers retreated, a second wave followed, raining more destruction on the already crippled fleet. By this time, the base was fully engulfed in flames. Fires raged on the USS *California*, the USS *Oklahoma* had already capsized, and the USS *Nevada* attempted to escape the harbor, only to run aground.[31]

The scene was one of apocalyptic devastation. Ships lay burning and sinking, bodies floated in the water. The air was thick with smoke and ash, survivors choking, struggling to find safety. The roar of explosions continued, punctuated by the screams of the injured. It was a picture of hell on earth.

By the time the attack ended, two hours later just before 10:00 a.m., Pearl Harbor was left in ruins. Twenty-one ships had been damaged or destroyed. Over 2,400 Americans were dead—sailors, soldiers, civilians—with another thousand wounded. Families were shattered and the island, just minutes ago a paradise, was now a scene of unspeakable grief.

News of the attack spread like wildfire. Americans sat frozen in disbelief as they listened to reports of the carnage. President Franklin D. Roosevelt addressed the nation the following day, calling December 7, 1941, "a date which will live in infamy."[32]

For the American people, the attack on Pearl Harbor was not just a military disaster; it was a deeply personal wound. The illusion of safety on the other side of the ocean from her enemies had vanished and the weight of war became real.

---

31 Imperial War Museums, "What Happened at Pearl Harbor?", https://www.iwm.org.uk/history/what-happened-at-pearl-harbor.
32 Franklin D. Roosevelt, "Pearl Harbor Address to the Nation," December 8, 1941, The American Presidency Project, https://www.presidency.ucsb.edu/documents/address-the-congress-asking-declaration-war.

Fast forward four years.

Though Japan had risen as a formidable military power in the early 1940s, occupying large portions of China, Southeast Asia, and the Pacific, by mid-1945, the tide had turned. The Allied forces achieved significant victories—the capture of the Philippines, the Battle of Iwo Jima, and Okinawa.

These battles demonstrated Japan's unwillingness to yield as soldiers and civilians fought to the death, reflecting the Bushido code of loyalty and honor.

Despite military losses, Japan's leadership resisted calls for surrender. The Allies, determined to end the war in a decisive, no-nonsense manner, issued the Potsdam Declaration on July 26, 1945, demanding Japan's unconditional surrender.[33] But Emperor Hirohito remained defiant.

On August 6, 1945, the United States dropped an atomic bomb on Hiroshima, obliterating the city and killing an estimated 140,000 people by the end of the year. Three days later, on August 9, a second bomb was dropped on Nagasaki, killing 70,000. These unprecedented acts of destruction brought the horrors of modern warfare to a new level and underscored the futility of further resistance by Japan.

Japan's leadership was forced to confront the inevitable. Her military resources were depleted, her cities lying in ruins, and her people suffering immense hardship.

In an historic moment on August 15, 1945, the emperor recorded a radio address to the Japanese people, announcing the decision to wave a white flag—to surrender.

---

33 United States, United Kingdom, and China, Potsdam Declaration: Proclamation Defining Terms for Japanese Surrender, July 26, 1945, National Archives,https://www.archives.gov/milestone-documents/potsdam-proclamation.

It was the first time most Japanese citizens had ever heard his voice. The formal surrender ceremony took place at four minutes past 9 on September 2, 1945, aboard the USS Missouri in Tokyo Bay. Representatives of the Japanese government signed the Instrument of Surrender,[34] bringing World War II to an end.[35]

The surrender of Japan led to significant changes for both Japan and the world. Under the guidance of the Allied occupation, Japan transitioned from a militaristic empire to a peaceful, democratic nation. The country adopted a new constitution, renounced war as a means of resolving international disputes, and put forward a plan focused on economic recovery.[36]

Culturally, waving a white flag challenged Japan's centuries-long ideals of honor and pride. While some viewed it as a moment of humiliation, others saw it as a critical step toward renewal. Japan's surrender symbolized the triumph of peace over conflict, though at tremendous cost.

Your Whole Life

One of the most important elements of pausing to truly follow Jesus is centered on surrender. Surrender is always costly. True surrender is about victory over defeat, obedience over rebellion, following over wandering away—at the price of your life.

---

34 "Instruments of Surrender," September 2, 1945, National Archives, https://www.archives.gov/milestone-documents/instruments-of-surrender.
35 National Archives, "Surrender of Japan (1945)," https://www.archives.gov/milestone-documents/surrender-of-japan.
36 "A day of infamy: Attack on Pearl Harbor: 7th December 1941," *The Second World War*, https://www.thesecondworldwar.org/the-pacific-war/pearl-harbour.

Believing in Jesus as Savior is free—salvation doesn't cost anything. Following Jesus as Lord is expensive. It requires everything you are. Surrendering to Jesus isn't about giving up something; it's about giving over everything—your whole life for your whole life.

Surrendering to Jesus isn't simply waving a white flag in the air. It is a beautiful act of defiance and rebellion to the system and values of the world around us, releasing control and submitting every aspect of life to God—decisions, struggles, desires, family, goals, resources, dreams, future—to His will and guidance. It is an act of faith, humility, and trust where you acknowledge that God's wisdom, power, and love are greater than your efforts.

It isn't about attempting to fix ourselves through a series of Bible studies and prayer points or striving to climb to the next upward rung of Christian maturity. It is allowing God access to the deepest parts of us, acknowledging He's our Source and allowing Him to meet us where we are, letting Him do what only He can do.

Still want to do it?

Pausing and surrendering are deeply intertwined. When we let go of control and give our lives over to Jesus, we create space—space for His healing and restoration and sanctification to take root in us. This act of pausing—of yielding—is not passive; it is an intentional decision to allow God to guide us into rhythms that nurture and sustain our souls.

"If anyone would come after me, let him deny himself and take up his cross daily and follow me. For whoever would save

his life will lose it, but whoever loses his life for my sake will save it" (Luke 9:23-24, ESV).

Denying yourself isn't a popular theme these days. We'd rather gluttonize ourselves, though we would never admit that. Whether it be with food or vacations, luxuries or resources or free time, refusing ourselves doesn't come easily. We prefer believing we are made for and have a right to excess and comfort.

Denial requires submitting and surrendering everything that's found upstream—putting God's will above our own, letting go of sin, resisting temptations that pull us away from Him, choosing to live sacrificially, serving others, being generous, submitting ourselves to others, expressing forgiveness where it is least deserved, loving our enemies, having a voice for the voiceless, prioritizing the Jesus Kingdom over personal gain. . . . SOMEBODY STOP ME!

Jesus said, "You must give up everything you have to follow me. If you don't, you cannot be my follower" (Luke 14:33, ICB).

No mincing words. Easy to understand. No interpretation necessary. Really tough to do. Everything.

Because money might come between you and God—and you have to choose.

A relationship might come between you and God—and you have to choose.

A particular job might come between you and God—and you have to choose.

A decision of integrity might come between you and God—and you have to choose.

Everything. Or you cannot be His follower.

Then ... take up a cross.

The place we most often see crosses these days is on gold chains hanging around necks—but they weren't wearing that jewelry in the first century, and that wasn't the picture that came to the early believers' minds when they heard that word. A cross was an instrument of torture and suffering—our present-day electric chair—our lethal injection. It represented the ultimate knockout—death and personal destruction in the most humiliating, public and brutal fashion.

This was a call to radical white flag waving, a willingness to endure genuine hardship for the sake of Christ.

"Blessed are you when people hate you, when they exclude you and insult you and reject your name as evil, because of the Son of man. . . . Woe to you when everyone speaks well of you" (Luke 6:22, 26).

"If you want to be my disciple, you must, by comparison, hate everyone else—your father and mother, wife and children, brothers and sisters—yes, even your own life. Otherwise, you cannot be my disciple" (Luke 14:26, NLT).

Your whole life. Or you cannot be His follower.

Sacrifice. Or you cannot be His follower.

Actual inconvenience. Or you cannot be His follower.

Sacrifice and inconvenience doesn't mean your Door-Dash didn't arrive when you thought it should, or online shopping wouldn't accept your credit card. It doesn't mean the Internet isn't working at the cafe where you decided to spend the afternoon, or that you hit all red lights on your way to the meeting you were already late to.

No.

Instead, it might mean facing personal rejection and misunderstanding. It might mean encountering unwarranted criticism for the godly values you're trying to live out. It might mean being excluded and spurned by those who don't know Jesus. It might mean rifts in personal relationships, workplaces, or online communities because of your faith stance. It might mean doing something unselfishly for someone at the end of a day when you're already wrung out.

||||||||||||||||||||||||||||||||||||||||||||||||||||||||||||||||||||||||||||||||||

One way to lean in to surrender is to remember God's past faithfulness.

||||||||||||||||||||||||||||||||||||||||||||||||||||||||||||||||||||||||||||||||||

But perhaps the most daunting part of surrender isn't denying yourself or even taking up a cross. It's that little word "daily." It's the consistency and commitment that "daily" requires. It's easy to have isolated moments of faith and lone instances of kind acts, but "daily" demands an uncommon discipline, an abnormal perseverance, and an unconventional reliance on God.

On Monday, we may feel spiritually strong, but by Wednesday, we are struggling with doubt. The call to follow

Jesus daily means choosing Him when we don't feel like it and when extraordinary challenges rear their heads.

One way to lean in to surrender is to remember God's past faithfulness. Someone said the best predictor of future behavior is past behavior. That holds true with our Father in heaven, the One who never changes, the One who is always faithful and true.

The bane of the Israelites was that they constantly forgot what God had done for them. They forgot:

» The parting of the Red Sea and crossing on dry land
» The drowning of the Egyptians in the sea behind them
» The manna that fell onto their plates every morning
» The water that sprung from a rock
» The cloud and fire that led them by day and night
» The Commandments hand-delivered to them written by the finger of God

You would think those events would be indelibly imprinted in their hearts and minds, but they forgot. We can identify. God has been good to us over and over, and yet we forget. Pausing to remember His faithfulness is key to the "daily" part of surrender.

"Jesus Christ is the same yesterday, today and forever" (Hebrews 13:8).

"Be strong and courageous . . . for the LORD your God goes with you; he will never leave you nor forsake you" (Deuteronomy 31:6).

"Every good and perfect gift is from above, coming down from the Father of the heavenly lights, who does not change like shifting shadows" (James 1:17).

"If we are faithless, he remains faithful, for he cannot disown himself" (2 Timothy 2:13).

Surrendering to Jesus is about trusting—acknowledging that God does best and knows best—leaning in daily to the teachings of Scripture, even the cringy ones.

Forgive your enemy. That's a cringy teaching.

Love your enemies. That's a cringy teaching.

Don't be conformed to the world. That's a cringy teaching.

Choose humility over pride. A cringy teaching.

Don't lust or be greedy. Cringy.

This kind of following and obedience is culturally counter-intuitive. Culture is not a peaceful breeze floating us to the feet of Jesus. It is a hurricane force wind sweeping us away from all that is holy and that truly brings freedom.

Holding onto unforgiveness—culture-intuitive—is applauded and encouraged by society. But it weighs heavily on the soul that is surrendered to Jesus. Extending forgiveness, which always feels undeserved—counter-intuitive—lifts that burden.

Fixating on grudges—culture-intuitive—gets celebrated. You were done wrong? Get even. Restoring relationships—counter-intuitive—brings the cleansing our souls desperately seek.

Gossip—culture-intuitive—is accepted and expected. Blessing and speaking words of life—counter-intuitive—are the ways of Jesus.

Racing forward into life to get what you believe you need and checking off your most ambitious boxes—all culture-intuitive things—is admired. Finding regular moments to pause so your soul can be fully surrendered—counter-intuitive—is the pathway to life more abundant.

Surrender begins here in the pause.

Abraham's Surrender

Abraham woke early that morning, the rising sun painting the eastern sky in warming colors of orange and pink. But the beauty of the dawn did little to lift the heaviness weighing on his heart. The words God had spoken the night before echoed relentlessly in his mind: "Take your son, your only son, whom you love—Isaac.... Sacrifice him as a burnt offering on a mountain I will show you" (Genesis 22:2).

Isaac was everything to Abraham. He was the child of promise, the son Abraham and Sarah had waited a lifetime for, living proof of God's covenant to make Abraham's descendants as numerous as the stars. Now, God was asking for him back. Abraham didn't understand. How could God's promise be fulfilled if Isaac was gone? Yet Abraham's faith in God's goodness was unshakeable. He had walked with God too long to doubt Him, even when it didn't make sense.

With trembling hands, Abraham prepared for the journey. He split wood for the burnt offering, loaded the donkey, and called for Isaac and two servants. They set out for the place God had told him. The journey was not physically strenuous, more a crippling passage of emotion, each step a battle between love and obedience. Abraham's mind brimmed with questions, but he resolved to trust God, even in the face of what seemed the impossible.

On the third day, the mountain came into view. He almost wished it would never appear, but there it was, reliable as the sunrise. Abraham paused to tell his servants, "Stay here with the donkey while the boy and I go worship and then we will come back to you." His voice was steady, but his heart was breaking. And yet his words held a quiet, desperate hope.

We will come back.

Isaac, young and strong and carrying the wood for the burnt offering on his back, walked alongside his father. His energetic spirit was undaunted and contagious and his boy-like curiosity broke the silence.

"Father?"

"Yes, my son?"

"The fire and the wood are here...but where is the lamb for the burnt offering?"

Abraham swallowed hard, fighting back the lump in his throat. "God will provide the lamb, my son," (vv. 7-8) he said, his faith holding even as his heart threatened to wrench itself out of his body. Isaac nodded innocently, trusting his father's words as they continued their ascent.

When they reached the summit, Abraham built an altar with tottering hands. He arranged the wood, each piece laid with care, taking more time than it deserved, and then he turned to Isaac. With tears in his eyes, he explained what God had commanded. Isaac, though confused and suddenly afraid, trusting his father implicitly, allowed himself to be bound. Abraham's heart splintered with every movement, but his faith held ground. He laid Isaac on the altar, his beloved son, the gift of God's promise.

As Abraham raised the knife, his heart cried out silently, Lord, please—if You're going to, now is the time—please! And before the blade could fall, a voice thundered from heaven: "Abraham! Abraham!"

"Yes, Lord! I'm here," Abraham replied, his voice trembling.

"Do not lay a hand on the boy," the Lord commanded. "I know that you fear God, because you have not withheld from me your only son" (vv. 11-12).

Abraham's knees buckled as relief and gratitude flooded his soul. He quickly untied Isaac and embraced him tightly, tears streaming hard down his face. At that moment, he noticed a ram caught in a nearby thicket. God had provided, just as Abraham believed He would, in the nick of time. He sacrificed the ram in place of Isaac, and the altar became a monument to God's faithfulness.

Abraham named the place *Yahweh Yireh*—"The LORD Will Provide" (v. 14).

As father and son descended the mountain together, Abraham's heart was full. He still didn't understand everything, but he knew one thing for certain: God was faithful. God is faithful. God will be faithful. Abraham's surrender had not been in vain—would not be in vain.

This is how surrendering to Jesus works. We hold onto our busted lives, trying to fix things on our own, delaying or refusing to trust Him. But as we let go and place it all in His hands, He takes our brokenness and turns it into something beautiful.

Pausing to allow this kind of Jesus surrender to take place in our lives is the purest form of soul care.

How to Surrender

How do we surrender, exactly? The way is realized by four postures: Conviction—Faith—Obedience—and Ongoing Submission.

1) A Moment of Realization (Conviction)
   » Surrender starts when we recognize our own strength isn't enough.
   » Example: The Prodigal Son realized he was lost and needed to return to his Father (Luke 15:11-32).
2) A Step of Trust (Faith)
   » Surrender requires faith and admission that God's way is better than ours.
   » Example: Peter dropped his nets to follow Jesus (Luke 5:1-11).
3) A Decision to Let Go (Obedience)
   » Surrender happens when we choose to obey God even when it's difficult.
   » Example: Jesus in the Garden of Gethsemane—"Not my will, but yours be done" (Luke 22:42).
4) A Daily Choice (Ongoing Submission)
   » Surrender isn't a one-time moment or action but a daily decision to trust and follow.
   » Example: "Take up your cross daily and follow me" (Luke 9:23).

Pausing to surrender is a continual process. It's hard—and it's worth it. That you did it Monday, doesn't mean you don't need to renew it on Tuesday. It's an everyday heart position that says, *Not my will, but Yours be done.*

||||||||||||||||||||||||||||||||||||||||||||||||||||||||||||||||||||||||||||||||||

Waving the white flag to Jesus means letting grace do what grit never could.

||||||||||||||||||||||||||||||||||||||||||||||||||||||||||||||||||||||||||||||||||

There comes a point in every soul's journey where you reach the end of your own strength. And with hands trembling or maybe just tired, you raise a white flag.

Not in defeat, but in surrender. They aren't the same. Surrendering isn't giving up. It's laying down your arms—the ones you've used to protect yourself, prove yourself, push through on your own—and saying instead, "Jesus, I can't carry this anymore."

The flag is waved not out of weakness, but out of deep courage. Courage to stop running. To stop fixing. To stop pretending you're fine. Waving the white flag to Jesus means letting grace do what grit never could. It's a sacred surrender that says: "I trust You more than I trust my own control."

And the thing is, God does not forcefully drag us into submission; He graciously invites us to surrender. And how more gorgeous and lasting by far that is.

*Do not offer any part of yourself to sin as an instru-
ment of wickedness, but rather offer yourselves to
God as those who have been brought from death
to life; and offer every part of yourself to Him as an
instrument of righteousness. —Romans 6:13*

This is rebellion—and this is where surrender begins.

A Prayer of Surrender
*Dear Father,
I come before You with an open heart, ready to lay
everything at Your feet. I confess that I've tried to do
things my own way, and I recognize my need for You.
Today, I pause once again to surrender—my worries,
my plans, my desires, and my fears. I give You control,
trusting that Your way is always better than mine.
Help me to let go of anything that keeps me from fully
following You. Teach me to walk in faith, to trust You
even when I don't understand, and to rest in Your
perfect love. Fill me with Your peace, guide me in Your
truth, and empower me to live every day for You.
I surrender my heart, my mind, and my whole life
into Your hands. May Your will be done in me.
Amen.*

PAUSE 5-5-5 HACK: Take five deep breaths, for five seconds each, every five hours. It's a simple way to slow down and reset.

||||||||||||||||||||||||||||||||||||||||||||||||||||||||||||||||||

1-Hour Soul Pause Application: Surrender

It's okay if you're unable to complete the entire practice in one sitting. Give yourself permission to move at a pace that's gentle and sustainable—soul care isn't a race, but a journey of presence and grace.

To embrace the beauty and import of soul care, find a quiet and private place where you can be fully present with Jesus.

Things to have with you:

» A Bible (paper or digital)
» Something to write with

You are encouraged to write in your book. By dedicating this hour to soul care, you align your heart with God's peace and presence.

Minutes 1-10: Self-examination

As we put surrender into practice, a first step before going any further is to search our own hearts. As followers of Christ, we should become experts at beautiful confession.

"Whoever conceals his transgressions will not prosper, but he who confesses and forsakes them will obtain mercy" (Proverbs 28:13, ESV).

"If we confess our sins, he is faithful and just to forgive us our sins and to cleanse us from all unrighteousness" (1 John 1:9, ESV).

Take a few minutes to really examine yourself. Ask:

» Is there anything preventing me from being completely present with Jesus today?
» Are there distractions that need to be dealt with—physical, mental, relational, heart distractions?
» Is there personal sin that needs to be addressed?
» Is there anyone I need to forgive or ask forgiveness from?

Prayer of Confession

Minutes 10-25:
Surrender to God for the Christ-follower is a daily act of faith, humility, and trust. Every day is different, but think about a typical "day in the life"—your life. What does it look like?

How do you typically encounter God in your daily moments?

Write your discoveries below. Think about how you *could* encounter Him during those times, how you would *like* to encounter Him, even if for a few minutes—as you're walking down the hallway at work. As you're commuting in your car. As you're doing laundry or at the gym. As you first awaken or before your head hits the pillow.

How do I encounter Jesus? How would I like to encounter Him?

When I wake…
Breakfast time…
Morning activity or period at work…
Lunch time…
Afternoon activity or period at work…
Evening…
Bedtime…

PRAY: Ask God to help you encounter Him more often in your daily walk. Surrender happens moment by moment. Begin by giving God control in one area of your life above, then expand as your faith grows.

Minutes 25-40:

When we acknowledge how Scripture speaks about surrender on every page, it underscores the priority of our obedience in caring for our souls.

Look up these scriptures and make a note at each line about how it helps you better surrender your soul and life to a God who loves you—and what God may be calling you to surrender.

- » Proverbs 3:5-6 (surrendering worries, plans, and struggles)
- » Luke 24:42 (surrendering your will to God's will)
- » Romans 12:1-2 (surrendering mind attitudes and actions)

Minutes 40-55:

The Prayer of Examen is a good practice for continual surrender. It originated with Jesuit St. Ignatius in the

16th century. He developed the prayer while writing the Spiritual Exercises in 1522 to help people develop discipline in prayer.[37]

Let's do it together. Go step-by-step.

1) Place yourself in God's presence. Give thanks for God's great love for you.
2) Pray for the grace to understand how God is acting in your life.
3) Review your day—recall specific moments and your feelings at the time.
4) Reflect on what you did, said, or thought in those instances. Were you drawing closer to God, or further away?
5) Think about your day tomorrow. How can you have expectation that God will show up?

MINUTES 55-60: The Lord's Prayer

A "cherry on top" after the Prayer of Examen is often the recitation of the Lord's Prayer.

Close your soul-care time with that prayer. Pray it slowly. Don't rush through it. Each line has deep meaning. If you don't know it by heart, you can find it in Matthew 6:9-13.

"Beloved, I pray that all may go well with you and that you may be in good health, as it goes well with your soul."
—3 John 2 (ESV)

---

37 Joe Paprockie, "Spiritual Exercises of St. Ignatius," *The University of Scranton,* https://www.scranton.edu/the-jesuit-center/spiritual-exercises-ignatius.shtml.

Song:

"I SURRENDER ALL"

by Judson W. Van DeVenter (1896)[38]

38 Judson W. Van DeVenter, "I Surrender All," 1896, public domain.

Chapter 7

Wait for It

"If you want to fly, you have to give up the things that weigh your soul down."
—Roy T. Bennett[39]

Each annual visit to northern Wisconsin for the silent prayer retreat would be an opportunity to pause for three whole days and just "be"—relax. Get in touch with God. Be restored and revived. Take an extra nap or two—one of the highlights of my season. Since that first retreat five years before, I knew the Holy Spirit would make Himself

39 Roy T. Bennett, *The Light in the Heart: Inspirational Thought for Living Your Best Life* (Roy Bennett, 2021), approx.. p. xx.

known, and I was excited about what God had waiting for me each time.

On one particular retreat year, six of our team members went together. The event had begun to attract the attention of our staff, something they now eagerly put on their calendar. A soul-care culture had been created at our church, and this was the "piece de resistance"—three days to press pause.

No talking. Heads down. Walk slowly. Mind your own business. Be with Jesus. And have fun.

Honestly, fun wasn't a prescribed goal, but when you're with five youngish cohorts, fun comes naturally. Someone came up with the idea that we spend morning #2 kayaking. After the a.m. teaching session, the rest of the day is usually free to hang with Jesus however you want to. We couldn't think of a better place to hang with Jesus than in a kayak, drifting quietly down a lazy river.

Though I had never been in a kayak before in my life—barely seen one in person—it sounded amazing. They convinced me.

This side trip was premeditated. We had circled up on day #1 before the opening "no talking" bell rang and conspired to meet on day #2 at a specified location, travel to several cabins in the area where there were stored kayaks, load them onto the truck, and launch them in the river at a designated spot. I wasn't sure this kind of getaway was in the retreat handbook, but these five were rebels, and rebels are so inspiring.

In an effort not to be total insurgents, we were going to accomplish the float without talking to one another. We were determined to keep the spirit as well as the letter of the retreat guidelines. The plan was to navigate down the river one at a time, one hundred feet or so apart.

No talking. Heads down. Slow floating. Minding our own business. Being with Jesus. And having fun.

The October day in northern Wisconsin was unseasonably warm and beautiful. Trees turning shades of gold, crimson, orange, and yellow served as a canopy above the river that sparkled an azure that beckoned your iPhone camera.

I had never been in a kayak before in my life.

I'm 6'5" and weigh in at around 190. Tall and relatively lean. But tall. Though lean. But still tall. This makes my center of gravity up around where your chin would be. As we began, I found the floating experience cathartic as the river carried us effortlessly downstream. The oars were barely needed except to occasionally keep yourself in the center of the flow. I was fifth in line, and I could see the guys in front of me, some with their faces upturned so the sun could warm them, others with heads bowed meditating. I had my Bible with me in the kayak, along with my retreat folder and iPhone. I snapped some pics of the guys who were drifting ahead of me.

Beautiful and serene. It was going well.

I had never been in a kayak before in my life.

A couple of my experienced friends had floated down this river on previous visits, and they had mentioned that there were a few sections that resembled Class I and II rapids.

I was unfamiliar with these classifications, but for the record, according to Google, Class I is "moving water with small riffles. Easy to float down. Little training required." Class II is "medium rapids with clear channels, assistance rarely needed."

Cool.

About thirty minutes into the two-hour long float, the first section of rapids appeared. The kind with small riffles that required little training. I could see some rocks jutting a few inches out of the water. Nothing to worry about.

I had never been in a kayak before in my life.

I noticed that kayaker #1 easily glided through and past the 60-foot-long section of rapids. No problem.

Kayaker #2 ... #3 ... #4 ... check ... check ... check. My turn.

I had never been in a kayak before in my life.

I headed into the section of "easy-to-float-down, little training required" rapids with utmost confidence, wielding my paddle like a gladiator (which, now that I think about it, may have been my issue). It didn't help. That second rock did what it was put there by the devil to do. It turned me sideways and, my arms flailing like an inflatable in the Macy's Thanksgiving Day Parade, flipped me over.

I don't know if you realize how much a kayak filled with water weighs, but it's a lot. Too heavy for me to upright by myself. A couple of my cohorts got out and waded through the pelvic-deep freezing water to my rescue and helped me turn the kayak upright, so it was navigable again.

They did all of this without speaking to me or to each other. We wanted to respect the spirit of the retreat. No talking. Heads down. Be with Jesus. (Help your brother.) Umm ... have fun.

Now realigned and each of us sitting in our individual watercraft once more, we set off again. A couple of my friends were wet waist down; I had gone under all the way. So that was fun.

I was so focused on regaining my pride and equilibrium that it took me a minute or two to realize I no longer had my Bible ... or my retreat notebook ... or my iPhone ... or the sandals I had on when I started this adventure. They were somewhere at the bottom of the river upstream from where I had now drifted. Some of the more seasoned adventurers had brought waterproof bags to put their stuff in. Since I'd never been in a kayak before in my life, I didn't know about that option, and no one educated me on it. They really love me.

The gravity and implication of those personal losses began to weigh on me—it was all I could think about—until I saw the next rapids. Class I had been "moving water with small riffles"—I really hated riffles by now, and what I saw coming into view looked like nothing less than the Gore Canyon on the Colorado River in early June.

I'll skip the details and get right to it. You're way ahead of me anyhow. Tipped over again. Brothers to the rescue again. Three of them this time. Upright. The next rapids. Over again. Four brothers now to the rescue. Upright. The next— well, you get the picture. I was running out of brothers.

Were we still having fun?

By the third dump, they were wet to the bone also, and now, the retreat agreement to be silent had been pitched out the window. Mercy took over because, by now, we were only seconds from the disembarkation spot and with no more rapids to navigate, I climbed to freedom, bare feet now on terra firma with nothing left but the clothes on my back—not even my pride was still attached. As much as I tried to make light of it externally, my ego was deflated. Though they would never say it, I felt I had ruined the excursion for everyone. We were all soaked, and as we loaded the kayaks into the truck beds and drove back, I was grateful that the group had returned to their retreat commitment to be silent. I stared out the passenger side window, but I imagined they were stealing entertaining glances at each other while I wasn't looking.

And I wasn't looking. Head down. No talking. Trying to be with Jesus. Hang the fun part.

They dropped me at my cabin at the campground, still a day and a half left to the retreat. I stayed there the remaining thirty-six hours—not attending the sessions or going to any of the meals. Sitting on the bed without shoes or a Bible or phone. Positioned in the center of the room like a prisoner, basking in my misery, munching on the chips and fig newtons I had brought for cabin snacks. Taking a bath in self-pity.

Then I recalled how the retreat had begun—that first session, before the drowning—a biblical walk through the power and presence of the Holy Spirit in your life. The black folder, now sloshing with the trout, had outlined a soul-care process to get in touch with that Voice, be filled with His presence, and experience His rich existence.

With no folder or iPhone to distract—now just me and Jesus—those final hours turned into a sweet and powerful pause in the presence of the Holy Spirit. He did not fail. He came—convicting . . . healing . . . restoring . . . guiding . . . comforting . . . loving . . . filling me in ways I would have missed at a "dry" retreat.

The word "kayak" is *persona non grata* in our team lexicon now, but if I'm being honest, it was one of the best pauses (and retreats) ever.

Guide/Convictor/Comforter

Perhaps the most monumental pause in all of Scripture is found in the Gospel of John when Jesus says to His disciples:

> *"I'm going away. But don't worry. I'm going to send someone else to you, and it's going to be better. You will be better taken care of—more fulfilled—more joyful. You will experience more of My presence and power without Me here. This new presence will cause your soul to soar." —John 16:7, author paraphrase*

This was a prophetic pause for these disciples. It's coming. He's coming. I'm giving you notice. Get ready . . . to wait.

I would imagine that was a blow to their curious ears. *It will be better? Better than having you here with us in the flesh, Jesus? How could that be? What or who could be better than You?*

I mean, if you had the choice of spending one hour with Jesus in the flesh or the whole month with the indwelling presence of the Spirit that you can't see? Pick one.

I know which one you would pick—the one we would all pick, given that choice. Don't lie to yourself. "I'd like door A, Alex."

But Jesus said this One who was coming would be better. He was talking about the Holy Spirit.

In a recent study on Christian beliefs by Ligonier and LifeWay, "evangelicals agreed, 59% to 33% that 'The Holy Spirit is a force but is not a personal being.'"[40] So more than half of Christ-followers lean in to the idea that the Holy Spirit, the third person of the Trinity, is akin to something out of Star Wars—Anakin Skywalker on steroids—or something like that.

And yet, Jesus said this was whom He would send to be with His first disciples in His physical absence—and still to us two millennia later—to guide us. Comfort us. Help us. Counsel us. Convict us. Intercede for us. Walk with us. Develop the fruit of the Spirit in us. Someone so personal. Better.

To reinforce His future intention, Jesus said to them, "Peace be with you! As the Father has sent Me, I am sending you." And with that, He breathed on them and said, "Receive the Holy Spirit" (John 20:21-22).

Not only will I send the Holy Spirit as your companion, by My breath . . . He will live inside you. Something dramatic

---

40 Joshua Arnold, "Evangelicals Earn 'F' on Beliefs about the Trinity," *Juice Ecumenism: The Institute on Religion & Democracy's Blog*, 8 Nov. 2018, https://juicyecumenism.com/2018/11/08/evangelicals-beliefs-about-trinity/.

will happen when you meet Him. He will fill you and be the power source that sends you into all corners of your neighborhood and world. It will be better.

In fact, Jesus said that with the Holy Spirit, we would do greater things than He.

Greater things? Do you mean we will heal more people in your name, Jesus? Give solace to more of the poor? Open more blind eyes? See more people delivered? Bring peace to more troubled spirits? Release more prisoners? Provide the good news to more souls?

Greater things.

But first you must wait until He comes. The waiting was important because Jesus wanted them to know they could not carry on His mission in their own power—they desperately needed to be filled with the power of the Spirit. He knew that, left to themselves, their personal agendas would take them down wrong roads and ultimately sabotage the will of God for their lives.

So, you must wait. And I promise you, it will be better.

IIIIIIIIIIIIIIIIIIIIIIIIIIIIIIIIIIIIIIIIIIIIIIIIIIIIIIIIIIIIIIIIIIIIIIIIIIIIIIIIIIIIIIIIIII

When we pause and wait on Him, the Holy Spirit promises to fill us up and send us out.

IIIIIIIIIIIIIIIIIIIIIIIIIIIIIIIIIIIIIIIIIIIIIIIIIIIIIIIIIIIIIIIIIIIIIIIIIIIIIIIIIIIIIIIIIII

I have the opportunity to meet with a lot of people as they navigate marriage, parenting, habit patterns, faith and doubt, and other life choices. A man came to see me one afternoon. He was someone I had given counsel to numerous times. We were friends. He was at a crossroads with his job, presented with two very different paths—one secure and dependable offering financial stability, yet at odds with his true passions. The other option riskier and more uncertain, but it resurrected things in his spirit that connected to a sense of calling that was hard for him to ignore. His body language spoke loud and clear as he shared, sitting on the edge of his seat as he recounted the latter opportunity—slumped back in the chair as he talked about the first. I prayed silently from across the room as he spoke, asking the Holy Spirit for wisdom and direction.

The Holy Spirit prompted me to read a verse from the Old Testament book of Isaiah: "Whether you turn to the right or to the left, your ears will hear a voice behind you, saying, 'This is the way; walk in it'" (Isaiah 30:21).

It was a call to trust God and not fear—to step out in faith. I couldn't decide for him, but we prayed, and he left encouraged.

The next day, he texted. He had received what he called an unexpected confirmation. Out of the blue, a mentor he had not spoken to in months reached out to say, "I don't know why, but I feel led to tell you to trust God with the unknown. Don't let fear hold you back." And then his friend shared a scripture with him: Isaiah 30:21.

The Holy Spirit was speaking loud and clear, using both this other friend and me in different cities at the same time to confirm what God was saying to this friend.

It will be better.

When we pause and wait on Him, the Holy Spirit promises to fill us up and send us out.

He does that in the following ways.

The Holy Spirit Becomes Our Convictor

"When he comes, he will prove the world to be in the wrong about sin and righteousness and judgment: about sin, because people do not believe in me; about righteousness, because I am going to the Father, where you can see me no longer; and about judgment, because the prince of this world now stands condemned." —John 16:8-11

This conviction is not condemnation but a loving call to repentance and growth. The Greek word *elegcho*, often translated as "convict," signifies bringing a person to the point of recognizing wrongdoing or convincing someone of something.[41]

Our souls thankfully embrace this. We are already convinced that we are sinners. Our consciences out us on that. We only have to recall last Thursday to know the reality of it, much less review the past year or ten. Sin separates us from God, making us enemies of the cross, and we always

---

41 "ἐλέγχω (elegchō)," in Strong's Greek: 1651, Bible Hub, accessed June 20, 2025, https://biblehub.com/greek/1651.htm.

would be if it weren't for the redemptive, sanctifying work done by Jesus on a cross.

The nemesis of our soul comes to condemn us by using lies, guilt, and shame to make us feel unworthy of God's love. Revelation calls him the "accuser of the brethren," meaning he constantly reminds us of past mistakes, failures, and transgressions to make us believe we are beyond saving. He twists truth, making us feel hopeless and unlovable, tempting us to deny the grace of God. He uses fear and doubt to make us question our salvation, persuading us that we can never change or that God is furious with us.

But Romans reminds us: *"There is therefore now no condemnation for those who are in Christ Jesus"* (Romans 8:1).

Condemnation is life-choking and pushes us away from Jesus. Conviction is life-giving and beautifully draws us toward Jesus. This means that while Satan accuses, the Holy Spirit, by His kindness, leads us to repentance and promises to fill us with the forgiveness and grace of God.

A young man in my church shared how he struggled with anger. After a heated argument, he felt an overwhelming sense of conviction. As he prayed, the Holy Spirit reminded him of Ephesians 4:26: *"In your anger do not sin: Do not let the sun go down while you are still angry."*

This Holy Spirit conviction and the man's willingness to recognize it led him to seek forgiveness and restitution and begin allowing God to heal his anger. It could happen no other way—only by the filling power of the Spirit.

Will you accept Him as your Convictor?

» Pause to become comfortable with personal confession and ask for the Spirit's help in overcoming.
» Pause to focus on scriptures that confirm Jesus's power over your body, mind, and soul.
» Pause to trust that transformation/sanctification takes time.

It will be better.

The Holy Spirit Becomes Our Guide

"When the Spirit of truth comes, he will guide you into all truth, for he will not speak on his own authority, but whatever he hears he will speak, and he will declare to you the things that are to come" (John 16:13, ESV).

The word "guide" in John 16:13 is the Greek word *odega*—a word that describes a tour guide or one who leads you on an excursion.[42] We spoke in an earlier chapter about how the Shepherd both leads and guides—and here it is again. The Holy Spirit cooperates with the Son to guide us.

On our trips to Israel, we have been captivated and amazed at the man who, at age eighty, had more energy than people half his age and led us from one holy site to the next for seven days, filling our heads and hearts with information as well as personal passion about his beloved land. He had been a former Director of Tourism for Israel and hosted dignitaries, politicians, entertainers, and VIPs all over the country for decades. His excited and proud voice rarely stopped ringing in our earbuds, whether walking,

---

42 Rick Renner, "The Guiding Ministry of the Holy Spirit," *Rick Renner Ministries,* https://renner.org/article/the-guiding-ministry-of-the-holy-spirit/.

standing, sitting on the bus, eating, or speaking nonstop to whomever would listen about the country he loved. There was more knowledge in his head than you could mine in twenty years.

Tour guides know the way—we trust them during our journey. They are skilled with the information and back stories about the attraction, far beyond what we can ever learn from Rick Steves or Wikipedia. They tell you where to walk and where to look and possess deep knowledge on the subject and its history. They bring to life whatever it is you are touring.

Odega describes the guiding ministry of the Holy Spirit in our lives. Jesus was informing us that if we are willing to listen to the Spirit and follow His instruction, He will be a dependable life tour Guide for us.[43]

The Holy Spirit can be trusted to understand the lay of the land. He's familiar with the potholes, the dangers, and the adversaries, and He has knowledge and wisdom on whatever it is you're trying to figure out.

The Holy Spirit leads us via the Word of God, helping us comprehend and apply Scripture to our situations. He guides us by providing wisdom and direction day to day. He speaks to us Spirit to spirit, prompting us to act boldly in faith, and warning us away from sin.

When we pray, the Holy Spirit grants spiritual discernment, enabling us to make wise decisions and separate truth from falsehood. He uses circumstances as well as other believers to confirm God's plan for our lives.

43 Renner, "The Guiding Mystery of the Holy Spirit."

As we pause to be with Him, His guidance brings us closer to our Father God and transforms us into the likeness of the Son and empowers us to live a life that honors Him.

Will you accept Him as your Guide?

» Pause to seek Him for wisdom before making decisions.
» Pause to listen to His inner promptings.
» Pause and stay sensitive to His voice through quiet reflection and meditation.

It will be better.

The Holy Spirit Becomes Our Comforter

I'm a big fan of comfort. I've learned it's way better than discomfort.

In my early adult years, I spent four years in Springfield, Missouri at a Bible College training for ministry. I met my bride-to-be there. A college kid is typically light on money, but when you've saved enough, one of the places you want to go is Lambert's Cafe: Home of Throwed Rolls in Ozark, Missouri.

I'm not sure "throwed" is a word (my editor let it slip through), but that's exactly what makes it an awesome place.

Lambert's is the epitome of comfort food. It's a place where Southern hospitality meets a minor food fight. Yes, the smell of the food is delectable. Yes, the portions are the size of a convict's last meal. But it's the throwed rolls that get you.

A voice booms from a server on the other side of the restaurant: "HOT ROLL!"

You turn your head just in time to see a golden-brown orb soaring above you like a comet. A seasoned diner reaches high in the air and snatches it mid-flight with one hand. If he drops it, not to worry—there's another one coming immediately behind it. The throwed roll is the real magic at a place like Lambert's, where playing with your food is encouraged.

Comfort. Our souls crave and seek it in whatever form we can find it—peace from worry, noise, expectation, pain, uncertainty, guilt, loneliness. That list could go on for days.

Jesus called the Holy Spirit our Advocate or Comforter—*parakletos*, or, "one who is called to help."[44]

"I will ask the Father, and he will give you another Helper, too be with you forever, even the Spirit of truth" (John 14:16-17, ESV).

Helper. This Divine Comforter-Helper reminds us we are never alone. Through darkest moments. In serious illness. When provision is lacking—anxiety, unrest, worry, discouragement at all-time highs—the Holy Spirit's presence provides solace for grief and replaces despair with joy. He provides our souls with an unexplainable peace that passes understanding. All this is evidence of the Spirit's work.

Paul writes in Romans: *"We do not know what we ought to pray for, but the Spirit himself intercedes for us through wordless groans"* (Romans 8:26).

---

44 "παράκλητος (paraklētos)," in Strong's Greek: 3875, Bible Hub, accessed June 20, 2025, https://biblehub.com/greek/3875.htm.

This divine assistance ensures that our prayers align with God's heart, even when we lack the words. The Comforter is praying for us.

Will you accept Him as your Comforter?

» Pause to invite the Holy Spirit in.

» Pause to make the Holy Spirit your first response when you experience difficulty.

» Pause to rest in the assurance that the Spirit is with you always.

It will be better.

IIIIIIIIIIIIIIIIIIIIIIIIIIIIIIIIIIIIIIIIIIIIIIIIIIIIIIIIIIIIIIIIIIIIIIIIIIII

"Wait for it..."

That phrase has been around a long time, but Neil Patrick Harris as Barney Stinson made it famous in *How I Met Your Mother*, as in, "It's going to be legen—wait for it—dary!"[45] It built suspense for the reveal to come.

The waiting... is worth it. The reveal... is worth it. HE ... is worth it.

Now ... ask yourself that question we asked earlier: If you had the choice of spending one hour with Jesus in the flesh or the whole month with the indwelling presence of the Spirit whom you can't see...?

It will be better.

---

45 *How I Met Your Mother*, Pamela Fryman (September 19, 2005; Los Angeles, CA: 20th Century Fox Television), Television.

Fill 'Er Up

We take the opportunity to travel abroad every other year in the summer, mostly to Italy and Germany. These are our favorite places on earth to hang out—we love the people and the ambience (and the food)—the passeggiata—the gelato—and my wife is Italian, so...

We aren't train people, mostly because we enjoy going off the beaten path to places the trains don't go, being free spirits with our itinerary. The first time we rented a car and drove through Europe, it was nerve-wracking—narrow, windy roads with motorized cycles weaving in and out through the smallest cracks in traffic.

Having a rental car in Italy can get a little complicated. Navigating tolls. Deciphering the constantly shifting speed limits and traffic signs. Preventing scrapes to your bumper in tight parking spaces. Translating kilometers into mph. Avoiding restricted driving zones. Figuring out how to pump and pay for gas.

‖‖

Getting filled up isn't the issue as much as what you fill yourself with.

‖‖

On our first trip, we rented the coolest-looking station wagon—station wagons aren't cool in the US, but in Europe

…wheeee!!! We had driven for about a week before needing fuel and stopped at our first gas station on a nearly empty tank, which is how I like to roll, much to my wife's chagrin, but that's another book. I was unfamiliar with the pumps but grabbed the one I thought was right. It just looked right. I had a gut about it. I did notice that the nozzle wasn't a great fit for the tank opening. I'm astute that way, but I helped it along by holding it at just the right angle so the gas could funnel into the tank. If you're not smarter than a fuel pump, well…

Having successfully filled up, we got back on the road, happily navigating to our next destination. It wasn't ten minutes into our new journey that the car began to sputter and shake, and in seconds, it had stopped in the middle of the road. It wouldn't restart, and we eventually had to call a tow truck to have it hauled away.

I'm sure you're on to me at this point. I had filled a diesel engine with gasoline.

Moral of the story: Getting filled up isn't the issue as much as what you fill yourself with.

First Century Pause to Wait

Pausing to be filled with the Spirit reshapes every aspect of life. When the Spirit lives in you, He brings more than the world can offer in a hundred lifetimes. He transforms you from the inside-out. Being filled with His presence provides everything supernatural—peace and joy, inordinate strength and wisdom, abundant presence and passion, extravagant kindness and compassion. His Spirit empowers you to overcome sin and leads you to live in a way that honors Him.

The earliest followers of Jesus understood the importance of being filled with the Spirit.

In Acts 8, we find Philip leading people to faith all over Samaria. Samaria—a place rooted in centuries of ethnic bias, religious disputes, and political rivalries. When the apostles heard this was happening there, they sent a delegation to Samaria that included Peter and John:

> *When they arrived, they prayed for the new believers there that they might receive the Holy Spirit, because the Holy Spirit had not yet come on any of them; they had simply been baptized in the name of the Lord Jesus. —Acts 8:15-16*

Peter and John laid their hands on the believers, and they were filled with the Spirit.

The same thing happens one chapter later after Saul (later called Paul) has an encounter with Jesus, and the Spirit speaks to a man named Ananias to visit the place where Saul is staying.

"Then Ananias went to the house and entered it. Placing his hands on Saul, he said, "Brother Saul, the Lord—Jesus, who appeared to you on the road as you were coming here—has sent me so that you may see again and be filled with the Holy Spirit'" (Acts 9:17).

Keep following that thread. Now that guy Paul (formerly called Saul) is full on living for God, telling people about the risen Lord. Everywhere. Antioch. Cyprus. Paphos. Perga.

Pisidian Antioch. Iconium. Lystra. Derbe. Phrygia. Galatia. Troas. Neapolis. Philippi. Thessalonica. Berea. Athens. Corinth. Ephesus.

|||||||||||||||||||||||||||||||||||||||||||||||||||||||||||||||||||||||||||||||||||||

It was their pausing to wait for the promise of the Spirit that changed their lives forever.

|||||||||||||||||||||||||||||||||||||||||||||||||||||||||||||||||||||||||||||||||||||

And there in Ephesus, he finds more believers and asks them what he had undoubtedly asked folks in multiple cities prior to Ephesus: *"Did you receive the Holy Spirit when you believed?"* (Acts 19:2)

This is Paul's grand pause. Hold on. Have you been filled with the Spirit?

Not, "Have you stopped sinning?"

Not, "Are you treating your wife right?"

Not, "Have you given sacrificially?"

Not, "Are you in a life group?"

But, "Are you filled with the Spirit?"

This is who they were waiting for when Jesus said earlier that He was going to leave them. Beyond the resurrection of Jesus, this is the great turning point for all of Christianity. The coming of the Spirit. Prior to His coming, the followers of Jesus were hiding in fear—one betraying Him, one denying Him, one doubting Him, the whole lot of them abandoning Him.

It was their pausing to wait for the promise of the Spirit that changed their lives forever. Because after they are filled by the Spirit we clearly see transformed rebels. A transformed Peter. A transformed John. A transformed James. Transformed disciples. Power-filled disciples. But not only those. Transformed situations. Transformed circumstances. New strength that seemed unavailable yesterday. Access to God they didn't have last Wednesday. Renewed energy. Fresh passion.

It will be better. And it is your pausing to wait for the Spirit that holds the hope and promise of changing your life for the better, too.

"But you will receive power when the Holy Spirit comes on you; and you will be my witnesses in Jerusalem, and in all Judea and Samaria, and to the ends of the earth" (Acts 1:8).

All because you leaned into the right kind of rebellion— and paused to wait.

|||||||||||||||||||||||||||||||||||||||||||||||||||||||||||||||||||||

A Prayer for the Holy Spirit

Holy Spirit,
Fill me with Your presence, guide me in Your truth,
lead me closer to Jesus. Keep my heart soft with Your
sweet conviction. I surrender my thoughts, my actions,
and my desires to You. Transform me, renew my
mind, shape my heart to reflect the love of God.

*Give me wisdom when I am uncertain, strength when I
feel weak, and peace when life feels overwhelming. Help
me to walk in step with You, listening to Your voice and
following Your Spirit's leading. Empower me to love others
as Jesus loves, to serve with joy, and to live boldly in faith.
Holy Spirit, be my Comforter, my Teacher, and my
Source of strength. Let Your presence dwell within
me, filling me with Your power and grace each day.
Amen.*

||||||||||||||||||||||||||||||||||||||||||||||||||||||||||||||||||

PAUSE HACK: Create "white space" in your life—block
out ten minutes in your calendar just to pause. No work,
no tasks—just a mental breather.

||||||||||||||||||||||||||||||||||||||||||||||||||||||||||||||||||

1-Hour Soul Pause Application: The Holy Spirit

It's okay if you're unable to complete the entire practice
in one sitting. Give yourself permission to move at a pace
that's gentle and sustainable—soul care isn't a race, but a
journey of presence and grace.

To embrace the beauty and import of soul care, find a quiet
and private place where you can be fully present with Jesus.

» Things to have with you:
» A Bible (paper or digital)
» Paper to write on

» A pen to write with

You are encouraged to write in your book. By dedicating this hour to soul care, you align your heart with God's peace and presence.

Minutes 1-15: Confession

The Holy Spirit is your Convictor.

Conviction is beautiful and normal for a believer and is the essence of pausing to care for our souls. It is not a heavy weight to be born; it is a freedom to be loved and embraced. The Holy Spirit helps us by identifying things in our lives that aren't like Jesus and then leading us to repentance and confession.

Confession is the pathway of approaching God with humility and then being cleansed by a loving Father.

They say, "Confession is good for the soul." First John 1:9 tells us that IF we confess, God is faithful to forgive us and wash us clean. IF.

What do you need to confess to God today? Typically, we think of the worst things we've done, and that applies. But think of things that have steered you from alignment with a Father in heaven who loves you. These could be:

misguided thoughts and actions—omissions (failing to do the right thing)—disrespect—unforgiveness— pride—greed—fear—passivity—lust

Where do you need to realign your life with Jesus today? Write those areas below.

_____

_____

_____

_____

_____

Now take each one by one and have a moment of repentance/redirection (i.e., determine to walk another way). Confess that Jesus is Lord of your life in that area of life.

Next . . . find a scripture that correlates with each to combat it so you can continue to have victory. Write the scripture references next to each above.

PRAY about them one by one.

Minutes 15-45:

The Holy Spirit is your Guide.

He lights your path and gives direction.

Read John 16:13 three times.

Where do you need direction: a job, a relationship, a present or future decision, something with your family?

Write below a decision that you are deliberating—small or large, it makes no difference. The Holy Spirit wants to be part of steering you day to day.

_____

_____

_____

_____

_____

Pause now to ask God for wisdom around that decision. What do you hear the Spirit saying, even if it's a simple nudge or impression? Practice hearing His voice.

The Holy Spirit is your Comforter.

Read John 14:26 three times.

Look up the scriptures below that affirm the peace and comfort of God. Meditate and reflect on each.

Jot beside each a couple of thoughts you hear the Holy Spirit saying to you as you read and ponder.

Philippians 4:7

John 16:33

Psalm 29:11

Romans 5:1

Minutes 45-60: Reflection

It is common to conclude soul-care moments with gratitude. Can you spend fifteen minutes in gratitude? Sounds easy, but...

What stood out to you during this soul-care time? Something was meaningful and memorable that you're taking away.

Recount and be thankful for what and how God spoke to you.

"Beloved, I pray that all may go well with you and that you may be in good health, as it goes well with your soul."

—3 John 2 (ESV)

Song:

SPONTANEOUS WORSHIP (Kevin Taylor)

Chapter 8

To Listen or Not to Listen . . . That Is the Question

*"God speaks in the silence of the heart.
Listening is the beginning of prayer."*
—Mother Teresa, paraphrase[46]

Surveys have asked: *"What would you like to be better at?"* Answers run the gamut. I want to be better at:

» Communicating
» Networking
» Caring for my body
» Forgiving others

---

46 Mother Teresa, *In the Heart of the World: Thoughts, Stories and Prayers* (Garden City, NY: Doubleday, 1986), [specific page number if available], in particular the reflection beginning "In the silence of the heart God speaks..."

» Public speaking
» Relaxing
» Tech
» Time management
» Resolving Conflict
» Laughing
» Forming healthy relationships
» Juggling (there's always one)

Know what I almost never see on those lists? I want to be a better listener.

The New Testament Book of James says, "Be quick to listen, slow to speak" (James 1:19). Seems we have that one turned around. Someone said you have two ears and one mouth, so...

I don't know that I'm a super great listener. I'm a good pastor-listener. Not sure I'm a good husband-listener. I guess that means I know how to listen, but I am evidently selective when it comes to good listening.

Joelene will ask: *"Did you hear what I said?"*

"What? Yes! Of course I did."

"What did I say then?"

Ever tried to create something in the moment and pray you were at least somewhere in the right hemisphere with your response? Mm-hm.

Or I'll say something, and she will answer: *"You realize I just said that very thing to you thirty seconds ago."*

"Yeah! It was so good I had to say it again." And that hemisphere thing replays.

I want to be a great listener, but it seems like a lot of work—and I'm a busy guy. Still, if we want to be successful at marriage and parenting and friendships and as followers who love God, learning to listen is key—and something we will never become proficient at unless and until we learn to pause.

God Speaks

One night in the quiet of the temple, a young boy named Samuel lay down to sleep. He served under the priest Eli, assisting in the house of the Lord. He lived in an age when God's voice was rare, and visions were uncommon.

As Samuel lay down to rest, he suddenly heard a voice calling: *"Samuel! Samuel!"*

Thinking it was Eli, he got up and ran to the priest and said, *"Here I am; you called me."*

Eli, confused, replied, *"I did not; go back to bed."*

Again, the boy heard the voice: *"Samuel!"*

Once more, he hurried to Eli, who again told him to go back and lie down.

A third time the voice called, and again Samuel ran to Eli. But this time Eli realized it must be God speaking to the boy.

Eli told Samuel, *"Go back and if He calls you again say, 'Speak, Lord, for Your servant is listening.'"*

Samuel returned to his bed. Then God called once more, *"Samuel! Samuel!"*

This time, Samuel responded, *"Speak, Lord, for Your servant is listening."*

From that moment on, Samuel followed God closely and ultimately became the last judge and first prophet of Israel, because he learned to discern God's voice from an early age.

Samuel was living out daily life when God called his name. In the same way, God wants to speak to us in the ordinary and every day. We seek Him so hard in the major events of life, yet it is in the routine environments Monday through Friday—washing dishes, changing diapers, walking down a hall, lifting weights, driving, shopping for groceries—that we need to hear Him just as much. More. These everyday environments shape our lives far more than the occasional big events.

Before Samuel could hear God, he had to pause to be still and listen. In our fast-paced culture, these intentional pauses help us tune in to the voice of God. But they must be more frequent than we currently engage them, because one thing is certain: God is speaking. Often. He is not withholding His voice. Stilling ourselves to better hear Him is what friendship with God is about because true and real friendship is built on communication, trust, and love.

||||||||||||||||||||||||||||||||||||||||||||||||||||||||||||||||||||||||||||||||||

That the Creator of a universe would desire any form of companionship with His creation is astonishing.

||||||||||||||||||||||||||||||||||||||||||||||||||||||||||||||||||||||||||||||||||

Much of our communication with God involves asking. Imploring. Complaining, even. One-sided and often self-focused. Communication based on friendship is two-way: Talking and listening. When we listen, we demonstrate that we want to know what God has to say. The more we listen to those we love, the more we come to know them and understand their hearts. Listening to God draws us closer and strengthens our bonds with Him.

Jesus said in John 15:15, *"I no longer call you servants, because a servant does not know his master's business. Instead, I have called you friends, for everything that I learned from my Father I have made known to you."*

Friendship with God. Those three words are stunning. That the Creator of a universe would desire any form of companionship with His creation is astonishing. And beautiful. Listening is key to that friendship. It's not as complicated as we imagine it to be. Listening can mean:

» Starting the day with a few minutes of quiet reflection. This sets the stage for the rest of the day.

» Turning off distractions like phones and media. This normalizes the practice of healthy silence and prioritization and heightens our awareness of His voice.

» Like Samuel, saying: "Speak Lord, your servant is listening"—this expresses an expectation and anticipation to hear His voice.

When was the last time you actually asked God to speak to you? And then paused for an answer?

Samuel needed Eli's coaching to recognize that it was God speaking. Before that moment, he hadn't yet learned to recognize God's voice. We can be so occupied or even unfamiliar with how God speaks that we can't hear Him. As with Samuel, we improve our ability to hear when we seek wisdom from spiritual mentors, mature Christian friends, and leaders who know what God's voice sounds like and can help us discern it when it seems unclear or dim.

Ask yourself: "Who in my life can offer the counsel I need to better understand what God may be saying?"

WRITE THEIR NAME(S) HERE: _____

_____

_____

Once Samuel recognized it was God speaking, he responded right away. He became fully dedicated from that moment forward. It was a defining moment in Samuel's life. When we know it is God speaking—whether by a thought, a word, in a conversation—taking immediate action sets us on a course that communicates a "yes" to Him. In fact, the more we say "yes" to God, the easier it is to say "yes" the next time. And the more we say "no" to God, the easier it is to say "no" the next time. Even a "maybe" is really a "no." Samuel obeyed God immediately.

Is your answer to the voice of God more often a "yes" or a "no?" And is it immediate—or do you delay? Note: Delayed obedience is disobedience.

It's beautiful and powerful that God called Samuel in such a personal way— *"Samuel, Samuel…"*—by name. God speaks personally to us as well. *"Kevin, Kevin," "Marcus, Marcus,"*

*"Sarah, Sarah," "Calvin, Calvin," "Carmen, Carmen," etc.,
(insert your name here).*

Our place is to expect to hear Him—and then be ready
and willing to obey:

» With our decisions: Before making one, take a moment
to quiet yourself and listen for guidance.
» In moments of tension: When you're overwhelmed,
pause to ask God for peace and next steps.
» With gratitude: Recall and reflect on times when you
have heard His voice in the past. He will speak again.

It wasn't just Samuel. Throughout the Bible, people
heard the voice of God in different ways:

» Adam and Eve heard the voice of God while walking in
the garden with Him.
» God spoke to Noah and gave instructions about
building an ark.
» Abraham heard the voice of God, telling him to pack
up all His people and stuff and leave home.
» A voice spoke to Moses from a bush on fire.
» Elijah heard a "still, small voice" at Mount Horeb.
» God spoke to both Jeremiah and Isaiah, calling them
to speak on His behalf.
» Ezekiel experienced the voice of God through visions.
» Daniel fell to the ground when he heard God.
» Saul heard Jesus's voice on the road to Damascus.
» John heard the voice of Jesus in visions while on the
island of Patmos.

God isn't done speaking to His children and friends. Jesus said, *"My sheep listen to My voice; I know them, and they follow Me"* (John 10:27).

When we speak of the voice of God, we are not talking about something you hear with the naked ear—not most of the time. The most frequent way we hear Him is through Scripture. "All Scripture is God-breathed and is useful for teaching, rebuking, correcting and training in righteousness" (2 Timothy 3:1).

His Word is His voice.

"And we also thank God continually because, when you received the word of God, which you heard from us, you accepted it not as a human word, but as it actually is, the word of God, which is indeed at work in you who believe" (1 Thessalonians 2:13).

Ignoring God's Voice

Not listening can have enormous consequences. One of history's most famous examples of that happened on the night of April 14, 1912. The luxury ship HMS Titanic on its maiden voyage, deemed unsinkable, was sailing across the Atlantic when it received multiple alerts about icebergs ahead. Other ships in the area sent at least six messages warning of dangerous ice ahead. These warnings were either ignored or dismissed as non-urgent by the captain and crew of the Titanic.[47]

---

47 "Failure to Act: The Titanic and the Ice Warnings," *Paul Lee,* accessed 19 June 2025, https://www.paullee.com/titanic/icewarnings.php.

Later that night, Titanic's radio operator received another iceberg warning from the Californian, a nearby ship. The operator returned the message: "Keep out; shut up, I am working Cape Race!"

Minutes later, at 11:40 p.m., the Titanic struck a massive iceberg. The ship many believed to be indestructible began to sink. Panic set in, and over 1,500 people lost their lives in the freezing waters of the Atlantic.

Had the crew and operators listened better and taken the warnings seriously, they could have changed course or prepared for an emergency—saving many lives. The Titanic disaster remains a tragic reminder that failing to listen can lead to catastrophic endings.

Sometimes, more can be learned by taking the reverse approach than the positive. The list of people in the Bible who listened to God is long. So is the list of those who ignored His voice:

» Everything begins with Adam and Eve in Genesis 3. They walked with God and knew what His voice sounded like. They ended by ignoring His direction and opened the way for the fall of humanity.

» Lot's wife (Exodus 19) was instructed not to look back as she and her family fled Sodom. She did anyway and was turned into a pillar of salt.

» Pharaoh (Exodus 7-14) refused to listen to the voice of God expressed through Moses, leading to his destruction.

» The Israelites roamed the desert for forty years expressly because they disobeyed the voice of God (Numbers 14).
» Samson (Judges 16) repeatedly ignored the warnings of God about Delilah's betrayal, ultimately leading to his downfall.
» Jonah (Jonah 1) initially ran from the voice of God calling him to preach in Nineveh. He ended up in the belly of a great fish for three days until he decided to obey.

The price these and others paid for ignoring God's voice is renowned.

How to Listen and Hear

Pausing to listen is subversive in a culture addicted to noise—rebellion at its finest. But it isn't enough to say: "Pause to be quiet and listen." It isn't a bad start, but how do we increase the likelihood of hearing God's voice?

First, practice listening.

Anything you practice is something you will become more expert at.

Make it simple to start.

Stop throughout the day—even for brief moments. Press pause—and listen. Really listen. Ask God to speak in that minute. Really ask. Set your phone or watch to alert you every hour on the hour. Just one small vibration on your wrist or ping from your device can be a reminder to pause and acknowledge that God is near and that He wants to speak. Imagine how adding fifteen more 60-second moments to every day would change your life and your ability to be sensitive to God's voice.

Simple, but powerful.

Isaiah 50:4 says, *"Every morning he wakes me. He teaches me to listen like a student"* (NCV). This means listening can begin as soon as you wake up, and that it is meant to continue without ceasing throughout the day until your head rests on your pillow.

Second, when you hear something, be sure the Word of God confirms it.

One of the enemy's great seductions is twisting Scripture to say what it never intended to say, as well as getting us to buy into the well-meaning (and sometimes not so well-meaning) advice from family and friends that can work against the truth of Scripture.

||||||||||||||||||||||||||||||||||||||||||||||||||||||||||||||||||||||||||||||||

Sometimes the hard way **is** the right way.

||||||||||||||||||||||||||||||||||||||||||||||||||||||||||||||||||||||||||||||||

"All flesh is like grass and all its glory like the flower of grass. The grass withers and the flower falls, but the word of the Lord remains forever" (1 Peter 1:24-25, ESV).

I can't tell you the number of times someone has come into my office, certain about something they believe God said to them.

It's probably safe to tell this story now, but many years ago, at a church we served, a husband came into my office to discuss his marriage. He was a long-time believer—had been in our congregation for more than a decade. With all I knew about him, I knew him to be a mature Christ-follower who believed and followed the Word. During the course of conversation, I learned he was leaning toward pursuing a divorce from his wife of more than twenty years. It seems we're often looking for the "out-clause" rather than leaning into redemptive healing, though hard solutions. Sometimes the hard way *is* the right way. We talked through some scriptures that I was certain he already had memorized, and to be honest, I had confidence that once we opened the Bible and examined it together, he would come around. We went back and forth, but at some point, it became clear that his mind was made up. He was going to divorce his wife.

At this point, I kindly yet firmly pressed him regarding the voice of God revealed through Scripture regarding his situation. It was not a matter of adultery or abusive actions or addictive behaviors. He simply did not want to be married to her any longer—said he didn't love her anymore—wanted someone different.

Finally, sliding the Bible that I had opened on the table between us his direction, I said: *"John (not his real name), do you believe this?"*

I could tell he was weighing the question as well as his answer. Then, at last: *"Yes, Pastor, but I'm still going ahead with it."*

"*But John, we follow this Word, not our own ideas. Your desires and plans are opposite to how God tells us to live our lives and lead our families. I know there's a lot of work to do, but this Word is God speaking to you. He'll help you, and so will I.'*

"*Pastor, I know what it says, but this is what I've decided to do. I'm going forward.*" I believe He heard the voice of God through Scripture. He was simply choosing to ignore it.

(This is the part of the story I'm hoping is safe now to tell.) I quietly brought the Bible back, got up from my chair, walked to my desk, and got a pair of scissors. I came back to my chair opposite him and cut out part of the page that offended him. I pushed the open Bible back toward him and said, "*John, is this the Bible you want to follow now?*"

I don't know for sure if God told me to do that or if it was just me.

He left angry, and I prayed I had not contributed to the demise of his marriage. Something wonderful happened in the interim—the Holy Spirit spoke—and the good news is that, at the end of the day, John did not divorce his wife. They spent months and years repairing what had been broken. But they kept at it, and God was faithful. And for those of you who are bothered by my actions, I understand. If it's helpful, I re-taped that section in my Bible when he left.

If it contradicts the truth of the Bible, it isn't God. No matter what.

Third, when you hear His voice, obey His voice.

Nothing improves your ability to hear God's voice like following through on what you hear.

God spoke to Moses and his people, saying:
If you fully obey the LORD your God and carefully follow all his commands I give you today, the LORD your God will set you high above all the nations on earth. All these blessings will come on you and accompany you if you obey the LORD your God.
—*Deuteronomy 28:1-2*

Later in the chapter, however, there are warnings for failing to heed the voice of God when you hear it. *"However, if you do not obey the LORD your God and do not carefully follow all his commands and decrees I am giving you today, all these curses will come on you and overtake you"* (Deuteronomy 28:15).

Be careful not to ignore the voice of God—and as you hear it, don't harden your heart to it (Hebrews 3:15), even when you don't like what He says. These are keys to cultivating a heart and an ear that regularly hears the voice of God.

S.O.A.P.

A powerful way to implement hearing and listening to God is through S.O.A.P.—a daily practice of being in the Word and waiting for God to speak. We make this a regular part of our local church and personal regimen.

S.O.A.P. stands for Scripture—Observation—Application—Prayer:

Step 1—**SCRIPTURE:** Select a passage of scripture to read. Read it through a couple of times.

Step 2—**OBSERVATION:** What do you observe in that passage? You can read a passage hundreds of times throughout your life, and God will highlight something different every time. What is God drawing you into this time?

Step 3—**APPLICATION:** What personal application from that passage can you make that impacts today?

Step 4—**PRAYER:** Pray that passage of scripture—you can't go wrong or pray wrong when you pray Scripture.

Then pause—and listen to what God is saying.

One other thing.

Sometimes people ask: "How can I be sure it's the voice of God and not last night's Chipotle?"

Romans says, "The Spirit Himself bears witness with our spirit that we are children of God" (Romans 8:16, ESV). This is evidence that, because you are made *imago Dei*, you have a built-in connection with God's Spirit. That isn't new age or Buddhism talking. Romans 8:9 tells us the Holy Spirit lives in us as children of God. And because we are His sons or daughters and are made like Him, sometimes those voices can sound similar.

Don't fret. There are a few principles that can help you determine the origin of the voice you hear:

» Does it come into alignment with the Word of God?
» Is it consistent with what you know about the character of God?
» Is it loving and grace-filled?
» Is it wise to do or believe?
» Can it be confirmed by a trusted, mature mentor?
» Would Jesus do it, say it, live it that way?

We can only imagine that each time young Samuel went back to his bed at Eli's request, he lay there in the quiet dark . . . staring at the ceiling . . . wondering . . . waiting—probably a little nervous—but expectant and a bit breathless at the possibilities.

Just like Samuel, we may not recognize God's voice at first. But the more we pause to listen, the more we'll hear Him, and the more we'll know it's Him.

|||||||||||||||||||||||||||||||||||||||||||||||||||||||||||||||||||||||||||

A Prayer to Listen to God

Heavenly Father,
In the stillness of this moment, I come before You
with a quiet heart. Teach me to silence the noise of
the world so I can hear Your gentle whisper. Help
me to lay aside distractions, doubts, and fears,
that I might be fully present in Your presence.
Open my ears to Your voice, not just in the moments
of prayer, but in the everyday rhythms of life.
Speak, Lord, for Your servant is listening.
Let Your wisdom guide my steps, let Your truth
anchor my thoughts, and let Your love shape my
responses. Grant me patience and clarity.
When I resist what You are saying, give me courage
and humility to obey. Above all, help me to trust
that Your voice leads to life and peace and joy.

Thank You for speaking through Scripture,
through others, and deeply to my own spirit. Help
me not only hear Your voice—but follow it.
Amen.

||||||||||||||||||||||||||||||||||||||||||||||||||||||||||||||

PAUSE HACK: Set your watch/clock to "ping" every hour on the hour that you're awake. This is a moment to simply acknowledge that God is real and that He loves you. If you're in a place where you can take a moment to be openly thankful, do it. This keeps you in connection with God all throughout your day.

||||||||||||||||||||||||||||||||||||||||||||||||||||||||||||||

1-Hour Soul Pause Application: Listening

It's okay if you're unable to complete the entire practice in one sitting. Give yourself permission to move at a pace that's gentle and sustainable—soul care isn't a race, but a journey of presence and grace.

To embrace the beauty and import of soul care, find a quiet and private place where you can be fully present with Jesus.

Things to have with you:
» A Bible (paper or digital)
» Something to write with

You are encouraged to write in your book. By dedicating this hour to soul care, you align your heart with God's peace and presence.

Minutes 1-10: Quiet

Listening is work. Its rewards are great.

Part of listening is getting quiet. In a world filled with noise, constant activity, and endless demands, it's easy to lose the ability to hear God's voice. The practice of pausing is an intentional act of stepping back and creating space for stillness—fine-tuning our spirits to God's gentle whisper.

Read Psalm 46:10, and then begin with ten minutes of nothing but "pause"—full-stop stillness—just you and God. *"Lord, I pause to quiet my heart before You. Help me listen for Your voice in this moment of stillness. What do You want to say to me today?"*

Embrace the discomfort of the "pause." At first, silence may feel uncomfortable and awkward. Resist the urge to fill it with words or even your own thoughts. Let it become a sacred space where God can work.

Shhh. Set a TIMER, and go for ten minutes.

Minutes 10-20: Respond

Coming out of that "pause," record below what impressions you got from God as you sat in silence and pondered His goodness and greatness. What thoughts and words were running through your mind and heart about God in those moments? What was He saying to you? Even if those thoughts feel small or trivial, record them anyway. This is how we train ourselves to hear His voice.

Then... set another timer. Ten more minutes. Sit and rest in these minutes.

Then... WHAT. DID. YOU. HEAR. HIM. SAY?

_____

_____

_____

_____

_____

_____

Minutes 20-30:

At the peak of the persecution of Judah by the Assyrians in the book of Isaiah, God has a message for His people. It is so counterintuitive, given the trouble that has consumed the nation: *"Thus said the Lord GOD, the Holy One of Israel, 'In returning and rest you shall be saved; in quietness and in trust shall be your strength'"* (Isaiah 30:15, ESV).

You've just come through twenty minutes of getting quiet and listening. During this time, it's still possible that the old patterns kept clawing at you. When things are stirring in life, quiet trusting is the last thing we want to do. But it's the first thing we must do.

What are the enemies that keep you from being quiet and silent these days? Maybe you were battling them moments ago. Name them below.

_____

_____

_____

_____

Take them individually and give them to God.

Minutes 30-50:
As the children of Israel are standing in front of the formidable Red Sea with the chariots of Pharaoh bearing down on them—between a rock and a hard place—God speaks through Moses. What He says makes no sense, and yet ... *"The LORD will fight for you; you have only to be silent"* (Exodus 14:14, ESV).

Just as inscrutable is the word God spoke through Joshua to the great-great-great-grandchildren of the people in Exodus as they faced their own Red Sea—except it was a huge wall this time: "Joshua commanded the people, 'You shall not shout or make your voice heard, neither shall any word go out of your mouth, until the day I tell you to shout'" (Joshua 6:10, ESV).

Jesus says: "Come to me, all you who are weary and burdened, and I will give you rest" (Matthew 11:28).

Rest is never noisy. Pausing allows us to experience the quiet He promises. We get fresh perspective for life inside the stillness. Priorities come into alignment.

How can you create moments in your day to pause to be with Jesus? Not as an exercise but as a pattern for vitality.

"Evening, morning and noon I cry out in distress and he hears my voice" (Psalm 55:17).

Think about your morning—your noon time—your before-bed moments. This is what Paul was referring to when he told us to "pray without ceasing." These scriptures indicate that not only does God want to hear from you all day long, there is a built-in premise that He wants to talk to you just as often.

Let's work through the day.

» Construct a morning pause moment to be with God. Ideas (pick one or two):

» Pray through the Lord's Prayer.

» Pause specifically with one goal: to listen to God.

» Confess.

Your idea _____

What would a pause moment at lunchtime or midday look like? Ideas (pick one or two):

» Read and pray through a psalm.

» Play a worship song.

» Use a scripture for S.O.A.P.
   (Scripture—Observation—Application—Prayer).

» Pause specifically with one goal: to listen to God.

Your idea _____

How will you connect with God in the evening or before you go to bed? Ideas (pick one or two):

» Express gratitude for what God did today.

» Use a scripture for S.O.A.P.
   (Scripture—Observation—Application—Prayer).

» Pause specifically with one goal: to listen to God.

» Prayer the Prayer of Examen.

» How did God show up in your day?

» Where did you miss God in your day?

» Pray for tomorrow.

Your idea _____

Decide to start today.

Minutes 50-60: Quiet

We bookend this hour with pausing to be still and listen. Now that you've practiced it here, it may be a little easier.

First Samuel 3:10 (author addition) says: *"Speak [Lord], your servant is listening."*

Sit once again in silence. Just listen. No need to write anything. Pause. Know what it means to be in God's presence with no other agenda but to enjoy Him. It might almost seem like time wasted—but there is no such thing when it comes to time with the Father who loves you.

Spend the final minutes pausing with God.

"Beloved, I pray that all may go well with you and that you may be in good health, as it goes well with your soul."
—3 John 2 (ESV)

Song:

"WHAT A FRIEND WE HAVE IN JESUS"
by Joseph Scriven (1855)[48]

---

48 Joseph Scriven, "What a Friend We Have in Jesus," 1855, public domain.

Chapter 9

Keeping Sabbath

"Sabbath is resistance. It is saying no to the culture of now."
—Walter Brueggemann[49]

We have been privileged to host tours to the Holy Land six times over the past twenty years.

Touring Israel is like stepping into a living, breathing history book, where every corner tells a story of ancient civilizations and spiritual significance, as well as 21st-century vibrancy. The beauty of Israel lies in its diverse landscapes but also in the layers of history, culture, and religion intertwined within its borders.

---

49 Walter Brueggemann, *Sabbath as Resistance: Saying No to the Culture of Now* (Louisville, KY: Westminster John Knox Press, 2014), rev. ed. 2017.

Jerusalem is a city that feels like the heart of the world to those who believe in Jesus. My wife is Italian, and during our trips to Italy, she has often said, "This feels like the home of my family." On our very first trip to Israel, she came away saying, "This feels like my real home."

The Old City of Jerusalem, marked by gates, cobbled streets, and historic walls, holds sacred sites like the Church of the Holy Sepulchre, Al-Aqsa Mosque, the Pool of Bethesda, the Mount of Beatitudes and Mount of Olives, Garden of Gethsemane, The Western Wall, Southern Steps, Via Dolorosa, and so many more, each one rich in significance for multiple faiths. Wandering through its ancient alleyways, you can feel the force of centuries of human encounters.

In the north near Jordan is the Galilee, centered around the Sea of Tiberias (Galilee), where Jesus spent a bulk of His known ministry and took a walk on water.

In the south, as you head toward Egypt, is Masada, Qumran, the location where the Dead Sea Scrolls were found, and the Dead Sea itself. The hotels that line the shore of the Dead Sea exist to pamper guests in the spas that beckon with their therapeutic properties of mineral-rich waters. The Dead Sea is made for floating. Since it is composed of 53 percent magnesium and 37 percent potassium, among other minerals, you can't sink in its waters even if you try. I was skeptical so I did try. You literally cannot sink.

Because of the timing and schedule of our tours, we often end up at the Dead Sea area on the Friday night of the tour.

Friday begins Shabbat across Israel. More than a religious tradition, it is an experience the entire country embraces. From sunset on Friday evening to nightfall on Saturday, the rhythm of life in Israel dramatically shifts as the day of rest begins.

As the sun sets, the call to prayer from the Western Wall can be heard, marking the transition to Shabbat (Sabbath). Streets become quieter and clearer as people gather for family meals. Shops close early. The city pauses. The air is filled with the sweet aroma of challah bread baked fresh for the occasion. Families gather at tables, lighting candles and reciting blessings over wine and bread.

One of the features of Shabbat is the "Shabbat shalom" greeting. It means "peaceful Sabbath."

The phrase is exchanged by friends, strangers, and neighbors, conveying a sense of unity and communal peace. Each exchange is a meaningful, if brief, friendship pause among the Hebrew faithful. Public transportation discontinues from Friday evening until Saturday evening. Streets refill with people walking to synagogue or just taking a leisurely stroll. Dead Sea hotel elevators have a "Shabbat lift" that automatically goes to the top floor and stops at every floor one-at-a-time on the way down so observant Jews don't have to "work" by pressing any of the elevator buttons.

Shabbat is a time to reflect—when people disconnect from the pace of life. They pause ... to read, pray, eat, rest, laugh, and sing together.

One of the most beloved Shabbat songs is "Shalom Aleichem," sung to the angels.

Shalom Aleichem

(שלום עליכם)

Shalom Aleichem, Malachei Hasharet,

(שלום עליכם, מלאכי השרת)

Shalom Aleichem, Malachei Elyon,

(שלום עליכם, מלאכי עליון)

Mi—melech Malchei Ham'lachim,

(ממלך מלכי המלכים)

HaKadosh Baruch Hu.

(הקדוש ברוך הוא)

Translation:

Peace be upon you, ministering angels,
Peace be upon you, angels of the Most High,
From the King, the King of kings,
The Holy One, blessed be He.[50]

***This is a perfect time to set the book aside for a moment and worship in your own way. "Shalom Aleichem" is a song. Pause here to settle in with a favorite worship song of your own before you move forward.

Sabbath Pause

To make Sabbath a regular practice in your life is the definition of what it means to press pause. If you make it here, you have arrived at a place where pausing is not a method, a stratagem or a gimmick, but a way of living.

---

50 "Shalom Aleichem (liturgy)," *Wikipedia*, las modified May 25, 2025, accessed June 19, 2025, https://en.wikipedia.org/wiki/Shalom_Aleichem_(liturgy).

You have wrestled your way through decision-making and priority-setting and chosen wisely.

Such a rebel. Beautiful congratulations.

The soul needs a Sabbath pause. It craves it. Constant busyness drains our energy, clouds our judgment, and deafens us to the still, small voice of God.

‖‖

We are different people going in to Sabbath than we are coming out of Sabbath.

‖‖

Sabbath offers the antidote.

It leads us to reconnect with God and remember that God is the source of everything we need.

It renews us, not simply by pausing from physical work, but by discovering the peace that soothes our souls.

It restores relationships by making space for family, friends, and community.

It shows us how to rediscover delight by engaging in activities that heal us and bring us joy and fulfillment.

In the creation story, God set the precedent. After six days of creative work, He paused, sanctified the seventh day, and called it holy (Genesis 2:2-3). God didn't rest because He was tired or because He needed a divine forty winks, but to model a rhythm of work and godly pause for humanity that was to come.

Sabbath was designed not as a burden or an obligation but as a gift—a time to rebel and step away from routine and experience restoration.

Jesus affirmed this when He said, *"The Sabbath was made for man, not man for the Sabbath"* (Mark 2:27).

Phillip Chan says, "Jesus is not against tradition; he is against tradition that yields no fruit." [51] We are different people going in to Sabbath than we are coming out of Sabbath. We are better people on the other side— filled up with the fruit that Sabbath and Sabbath only provides. You cannot reap that fruit any other way. Just Sabbath.

Honoring Shabbat

It is helpful to view how some of the original recipients of Shabbat, the Jews, honor and practice this weekly and holy pause still today.

Preparation for Shabbat

Preparation begins well before sundown on Friday:

1) **Cleaning and Cooking:** Homes are swept, meals are prepared, and everything is set in place so that no work will need to be done during Shabbat.

2) **Challah Bread:** Special braided bread is baked or purchased for Shabbat meals.

3) **Candles:** Candlesticks are set out, ready to welcome the sacred pause.

---

51 Phil Chan, "Explaining 'the Sabbath was made for man': 3 Massive Implications," *Phil Chan,* https://phillipchan.org/the-sabbath-was-made-for-man/.

The preparation itself is a spiritual practice—it serves to create a peaceful, welcoming atmosphere in the home.[52]

Welcoming Shabbat (Friday Evening)
Shabbat is celebrated with specific rituals and prayers:
1) **Lighting Candles:** The woman of the household typically lights two candles shortly before sunset and recites a blessing, marking the official start of Shabbat.
2) **Kiddush:** The family gathers for a festive meal beginning with the Kiddush prayer, a sanctification of the day recited over a cup of wine.
3) **Blessing the Children:** Parents often bless the children, asking God to protect and guide them.
4) **Challah and Meal:** The blessing over the challah bread is recited, and a leisurely meal follows. The family sings traditional songs and shares Torah teachings and stories.[53]

Observing the Day of Rest (Saturday)
On Saturday, Shabbat continues with restful, meaningful family activities:
1) **Synagogue Services:** Many Jews attend synagogue in the morning to pray, hear the Torah read, and gather with the community of faith.
2) **Torah Study:** Shabbat is considered an ideal time for studying Torah, engaging in discussion, and deepening one's understanding of the teachings.

52 "Preparing for Shabbat," *Chabad.org,* accessed June 23, 2025, https://www.chabad.org/library/article_cdo/aid/257741/jewish/Preparing-for-Shabbat.htm.
53 "Shabbat Evening Home Ritual," *Judaism 101,* accessed June 20, 2025, https://www.jewfaq.org/prayers_shabbat.

3) **Rest and Family Time:** Work is strictly avoided. Cooking and writing are traditionally prohibited. Time is spent reading, talking, and enjoying each other's company.

4) **Meals:** A second festive meal is shared after synagogue services, often followed by a good nap.

Havdalah: Saying Goodbye to Shabbat (Saturday Evening)

As Shabbat draws to a close, it is marked by the Havdalah ceremony, which separates the holy day from the ordinary week:

1) **Blessings:** Havdalah includes blessings over a cup of wine, a fragrant spice box, and a braided candle. The spices symbolize carrying the sweetness of Shabbat into the week ahead.

2) **A Song of Farewell:** Traditional songs are sung to bid farewell to Shabbat, asking for blessings in the coming week.

3) **Honoring the Week Ahead:** The candle is extinguished, and Shabbat ends as the first stars appear in the sky and the anticipation for the next Shabbat begins to grow all over again.[54]

For Jews, Shabbat is a cornerstone of faith, identity, and national rhythm. It is a weekly reminder of creation, liberation (the Old Testament Exodus account), and eternal covenant with God.

---

54 Susan Silverman, "Havdalah: Taking Leave of Shabbat," accessed June 23, 2025, https://www. myjewishlearning.com/article/havdalah-taking-leave-of-shabbat/.

What about today?

Honoring the Sabbath in the 21st Century

We tangle up everything. We don't need to. Sabbath doesn't have to be complicated. Your days are probably very full. You're juggling family and responsibilities and job requirements and home needs and a hundred other things—people are relying on you. Me too.

Pausing to honor God with Sabbath isn't easy—especially when the world keeps moving while you're trying to slow down.

Sabbath isn't about increased pressure or greater performance. It's about permission. Permission to breathe. Permission to be still for a few minutes. Permission to protest culture. Permission to believe that you don't have to be the one always holding everything together. God is.

Even if it's just a Sabbath hour to begin with, that's a beautiful start. If you don't fulfill a textbook rest day, that doesn't mean you failed. It means you're human—and that's exactly why Sabbath was made for you.

Take it one step at a time. God honors the desire and the attempt more than the checked box.

As a trial run, take one or two things the list below to begin:

1) **Set a boundary.** Choose a day or a portion of a day that you can regularly set aside and prioritize to unplug—from work, emails, media. Commit to protecting this time as sacred.

2) **Engage in family worship.** Attend a church service, read Scripture, spend time in godly meditation,

journal, and prayer. Center your day on the presence and goodness of God.

3) **Share a special meal.** Have a traditional meal with favorite recipes, set the table with the special dishware, and eat together without distractions. Alternatively, order takeout.

4) **Practice gratitude.** Reflect on the blessings of the week. Share thanksgiving with family and friends. Deepen your sense of shalom and contentment by reflecting on how good God has been to you.

5) **Do what restores you.** What makes you happy? A walk in nature, reading a book, enjoying a hobby? Unplug from technology. Sabbath pause may look different for everyone. Engage in people and things that bring life and refreshment.

6) **Perform acts of service and kindness.** Visit the sick, elderly, or someone in need. Write encouraging notes to friends or family members.

7) **Slow down.** Allow yourself to move at a more leisurely pace. Do everything "slower." Eat meals slower, walk slower, think slower, enjoy the luxury of unhurried moments.

8) **Close out with reflection.** Have a short family worship moment to thank God for the day. Share lessons learned. End with a prayer asking for God's presence in the coming week.

Here is a sample plan for a modern Sabbath observance.

Preparation (Day Before Sabbath)

» **Plan Meals:** Prepare meals in advance to minimize cooking and unnecessary work.

» **Tidy Up:** Organize your space so you can enjoy a peaceful atmosphere.

» **Tech Detox Prep:** Set up auto-reply for emails and texts.

» **Think about Activities:** Plan how you'll spend the day meaningfully (reading, walks, family time/games).

Sabbath Begins (Evening Before)

» **Candle Lighting:** Light a candle to signal the start of Sabbath.

» **Gratitude:** Reflect on the past week, expressing gratitude.

» **Power Down:** Turn off devices to fully engage in rest.

» **Shared Meal:** Have a special meal with family and/ or friends.

Sabbath Day

Morning: Quiet and Jesus Focus

» Begin with meditation, prayer, Scripture reading.

» Have a leisurely and healthy breakfast.

» Take a nature walk.

Midday: Community and Connection

» Spend time with loved ones in meaningful conversation/activity.

» Engage in acts of kindness.

» Journal thoughts and insights.

Afternoon: Rest and Recreation
  » Read an uplifting book or listen to good music.
  » Enjoy a creative hobby.
  » Take a nap.

Evening: Reflection and Closure
  » Reflect on the beauty of the day.
  » Express gratitude.
  » End with a godly ritual (prayer, song, or a period of silence).

Next Day Re-Entry
  » Ease back into regular activities with godly mindfulness.
  » Carry the Sabbath spirit into the new week by incorporating elements of rest and reflection into every day.

|||||||||||||||||||||||||||||||||||||||||||||||||||||||||||||||||||||||||||||||||||||||||

When it comes to living a life that fulfills the call to regularly pause, Sabbath observance may be as silver as any bullet gets.

|||||||||||||||||||||||||||||||||||||||||||||||||||||||||||||||||||||||||||||||||||||||||

Sabbath pause is a Biblical, godly rebellion against everything the world throws at you. In a society that glorifies hustle and measures worth by endless production, Sabbath is a stake in the ground. It is a battle cry and declaration that our value isn't tied to what we do but to who we are as children of God. When we pause to Sabbath, we're saying, *"Enough, world. I hope in God."* You can un-tense your shoulders and unclench your jaw. God has it.

The writer of Hebrews said, *"There remains, then, a Sabbath—rest for the people of God; for anyone who enters God's rest also rests from their works, just as God did from his"* (Hebrews 4:9-10).

This pause God calls us into is a break from carrying the weight of guilt or shame; it is a repose from the endless pursuit of trying to earn God's favor or the favor of those around us and an invitation to freedom. As John said in his Gospel: *"If the Son sets you free, you will be free indeed"* (John 8:36).

When it comes to living a life that fulfills the call to regularly pause, Sabbath observance may be as silver as any bullet gets, the one practice, if we will seize it, that has the power to reshape our lives more than any other—the one practice that defines caring for our souls like no other—the one practice that best shows us what rebelling to be with Jesus is truly about.

This beautiful rhythm of grace invites you to stop and start. Stop striving, stop worrying, stop carrying so much—and start being present, start acknowledging that you are deeply loved, accepted, forgiven, and welcomed into the arms of God.

Sabbath rest isn't retreat. It is resistance. It is an act of courageous faith. It is a way of saying, "God, I trust You to provide. I trust You to sustain me. I trust You to be enough."

Press pause and Sabbath. Your soul will thank you.

Parable of the Overworked Carpenter

Once upon a time, in a bustling village nestled in the shadow of a great mountain, lived a carpenter named Elias. Known far and wide for his craftsmanship, Elias was the area's sought-after artisan for furniture, tools, and repairs. It seemed he worked from sunrise to sunset, tireless, but also driven by the demands of his customers and his desire to provide for his family.

Elias prided himself on his work ethic, but over time, his days blurred into a never-ending haze of sawdust and deadlines. His hands grew calloused, his back ached, and his mind raced even when he sought the comfort of his bed. Despite wanting to slow down, he couldn't.

"If I slow down, even a little, everything will fall apart."

One day, a traveler arrived in the village. He was an elderly man with a calm demeanor, a gray beard, and a twinkle in his eye. He sat near Elias's open shop and watched him work for hours, observing his frantic pace. Finally, he approached and said, *"Your work is admirable, but why do you toil without rest? I have been watching you for hours, and you've barely paused even for a moment.'*

Elias wiped sweat from his brow and replied, *"There's no time to rest. People depend on me, and there's always more to do. I must keep going."*

The traveler smiled gently and said, *"Let me tell you a story."*

He shared the tale of two woodcutters. Both were tasked with chopping as much wood as they could in a single day.

The first worked tirelessly without pause, chopping away from dawn to dusk. The second, however, stopped every hour to rest and sharpen his axe. At the end of the day, the second woodcutter had far outpaced the first.

"Do you see?" the traveler asked. *"The first woodcutter spent all his energy swinging a dull axe, while the second understood that rest and renewal are part of the work."*

Elias frowned. *"But if I stop, I'll fall behind. There's no time to rest."*

The traveler's eyes sparkled. *"Ah, but the rest is not waste—it is wisdom. The time to pause is a gift, a time to sharpen your axe, refresh your spirit, and remember that your worth isn't tied to how much you got done today."*

Elias pondered the traveler's words but remained unconvinced. *"I'll think about it,"* and he returned to his workbench.

The stranger moved on. Weeks passed while Elias continued his relentless pace. One day, while carrying a heavy beam, he stumbled and injured his hand. Unable to work because of it, he had no choice but to sit down and stop working. At first, the forced idleness frustrated him. But as the days went on, he noticed something unexpected.

He began to hear the laughter of his children, the song of the birds, the jingle of the tradesmen handling their coins. He had time to share meals with his family, to think and listen, to pray. Slowly, he realized how much he had been missing in his pursuit of work.

When his hand healed, Elias decided to try something new. Every seventh day, he would set down his tools and honor Sabbath. At first it felt strange, counterproductive even. But over time, he noticed a change, subtle at first, then more evident. His mind was clearer, his body stronger, his heart lighter, his joy quicker to come to the surface. His work actually improved, and so did his relationships.

Months later, the traveler returned to the village and found Elias smiling as he carved an intricate chair. *"Ah,"* said the traveler, *"I can tell by your face that you've learned the rhythm of rest."*

Elias nodded. *"Sabbath has taught me that pausing to rest isn't a break from life—it's the fuel for it."*

Every Sabbath from that point on, he laid down his tools, grateful for the rhythm of work and rest that brought life to his soul.

> *If you watch your step on the Sabbath*
> *and don't use my holy day for personal advantage,*
> *if you treat the Sabbath as a day of joy,*
> *GOD's holy day as a celebration,*
> *if you honor it by refusing 'business as usual,'*
> *making money, running here and there—*
> *Then you'll be free to enjoy GOD!*
> *Oh, I'll make you ride high and soar above it all.*
> —*Isaiah 58:13-14 (MSG)*

Pausing to Sabbath reminds us that our value is not in our work but in the God who loves us.

||||||||||||||||||||||||||||||||||||||||||||||||||||||||||||||||||||||||||

A Prayer for Sabbath

Dear Father,
With a heart full of gratitude, I come before You on this
Sabbath day. Thank You for the gift of rest, for the sacred
time to pause from the busyness of life and dwell in Your
grace and love. It's a pleasure to just sit with You today.
Thank You for the breath in my lungs, the peace in
my soul, and the light of Your truth that guides me
every single week. I purposely set aside my agenda, my
worries, and my burdens, and I embrace the joy that
only You can provide. I put my faith in the renewal I
know You will bring. May this Sabbath be a time of
refreshing, reflection, and communion with You.
Bless my family, my friends, and all who seek You today.
May our hearts be drawn closer to You, and may Your
love shine through us. Let this day be filled with worship
and a renewed commitment to walk in Your truth.
Thank You, Lord, for the assurance of Your promises. You
are good. May this Sabbath be a way to honor You, and let
it be a foretaste of the future rest we will share with You.
Amen.

||||||||||||||||||||||||||||||||||||||||||||||||||||||||||||||||

PAUSE HACK: The floor is an incredible place to reset. Do it. Lie down on your back and enjoy the moment until you're ready to get up. You'll thank yourself.

||||||||||||||||||||||||||||||||||||||||||||||||||||||||||||||||

Soul Pause Application: Sabbath

Here is a sample day for your Sabbath pause.

Morning:

» Sleep in a little longer without feeling guilty. Thank God for the gift of Sabbath and invite Him to guide your day. Begin the day with quiet meditation.

» Enjoy a leisurely breakfast with your family or a friend. Use the time to look forward to what the day before you holds.

» Consider a "digital detox," intentionally disconnecting from screens and devices to focus on relationships and spiritual and mental health. A "phone-free" day for the entire family.

» Attend a church service or spend time reading Scripture. Allow worship music to center your heart and mind on God's presence.

Afternoon:

» Share a meal with someone. Prepare something simple yet special in advance to mark the day, maybe a family recipe or a favorite dish.

» Go for a walk or spend time outdoors. Soak in God's creation. The beauty of nature can be deeply restorative.

» Engage in a hobby or activity that makes your soul happy—reading, painting, gardening, golfing, swimming, fill-in-the-blank.

Evening:

» Keep the pace slow. Practice moments of gratitude.

» Share a moment of connection with family and loved ones through conversation, game playing, or simply being together. FaceTime out-of-town loved ones (your one exception to using your device).

» End the day as you began—thanking God for the treasure of Sabbath pause and asking for His peace to carry you into the new week.

NOTE: For ultra-busy weeks, consider a shortened Sabbath or an adjusted timeframe. Celebrate a "mini-Shabbat," focusing on Friday night dinner with family and carving out specific hours in the day or weekend where you can slow and reflect.

"Beloved, I pray that all may go well with you and that you may be in good health, as it goes well with your soul."
—3 John 2 (ESV)

Song:

"GREAT IS THY FAITHFULNESS"
by Thomas O Chisholm (1923)[55]

---

55 Thomas O. Chisolm, "Great is Thy Faithfulness" by Thomas O. Chisolm and William Runyan, 1923, hymn.

Chapter 10

Carousel Got It Right

"The need for connection and community is primal, as fundamental as the need for air, water, and food."
—Dean Ornish, Attributed[56]

In the town of Capernaum, word spread quickly—Jesus was back. He was visiting a family on the outskirts of town, and people rushed to the house where He was staying. Eager to hear His teaching, the house was soon so full that people stood outside, pressing against the walls, trying to catch a glimpse of Him.

---

56 Dean Ornish, attributed. "The need for connection and community is primal, as fundamental as the need for air, water, and food."

Not far away, four men carried their friend, a man who was paralyzed and unable to walk, on a cot. They had heard of Jesus's miracles and believed He could heal their friend. But when they arrived at the house, their hearts sank. The crowd was so large that they couldn't get anywhere near Jesus. There was no way to even get through the door.

Most people would have given up and turned back. Not these four.

Determined to take action, they looked to the left and then to the right—bodies everywhere. Then they looked up—and a plan formed. Carefully, they carried their friend up the outer steps of the house to the roof. Homes like these in the first century often had outside access to the top of the house for cooking and washing. The roof space could be used as another room in the house. Families might sleep out under the stars. In summer evenings, temperatures in the desert country were cooler outside than they were indoors.

The four friends began to methodically remove the tiles, thatch, and animal hides covering the house's roof, digging to create an opening. Dust and straw fell into the room below where Jesus was teaching.

A hole began to form, and suddenly, a mat was being lowered through the opening, and on it, the paralyzed friend. The crowd gasped and murmured at what they were seeing unfold right in front of them. The listeners inside and outside the house fell silent—watching—waiting.

Jesus looked up. He saw the faces of the four friends peering down, their eyes filled with hope and determination.

He couldn't help but smile. He saw their faith. He knew what was coming next. The mat settled right in front of Him.

Turning to the paralyzed man, Jesus said, "Son, your sins are forgiven."

It wasn't what the man was hoping for, nor were these the kind of words ever spoken outside the temple—and certainly not by someone who didn't represent the clergy of the day. Forgiveness of sins was restricted to designated spiritual leaders at designated spiritual places within the temple—not here. Some in the crowd whispered among themselves, questioning His words. But Jesus, knowing their thoughts, spoke again—this time saying words the paralyzed man understood completely: "Get up, take your mat, and walk."

At that moment, strength returned to the man's legs. He stood for the first time in years. The crowd drew in their collective breath in amazement as the man picked up his bed and walked out the door—healed—his friends above high-fiving one another in unrestrained victory.

But the healing of the man on the mat wasn't the only miracle that day. The catalyst for the miracle was the faith and love of his four brothers who refused to give up until their friend was made well.

This account is given in three of the Gospels and is a powerful example of community, friendship, and faith. The paralyzed man could not get to Jesus on his own—his bros carried him, dug for him, fought for him, and made sure he got the help he needed.

There is nothing more healing to our souls than knowing someone cares about us and will go to great lengths to see us restored, blessed, helped, encouraged—healed.

At least three things stand out in this account that impact the deepest part of us:

Pause to walk through life with others.

Broadway composers Rodgers and Hammerstein underscored the importance of community. Their famous song, "You'll Never Walk Alone," that premiered in their 1945 musical *Carousel*, told the story of victory in times of struggle with the help of those we love.[57]

More than forty years later, in 1989, hundreds of people were injured at a Football Association Challenge Cup game in Sheffield, England, when spectators rushed from the stadium, and people were crushed by the masses. Ninety people were killed. At the memorial service, attended by thousands, "You'll Never Walk Alone" was sung by a choir boy in an emotional presentation that honored the victims of that community.[58]

Fast-forward thirty more years. COVID-19 was running rampant globally. United Kingdom personality, Captain Sir Tom Moore, a British Army officer for much of his life, recorded a version of the song on the run up to his 100th birthday as a fundraiser for the National Health Service. It was the top-selling single of 2020 in that country. He is the oldest person to accomplish such a musical achievement.

57 Rodgers, Richard, and Oscar Hammerstein II. *Carousel*. New York: Williamson Music, 1945.
58 "Hillsborough disaster," *Wikipedia*, last modified May 31, 2025, accessed June 19, 2025, https://en.wikipedia.org/wiki/Hillsborough_disaster.

The song went on to be the most often performed song at funerals in the UK that year.[59]

The song that premiered in a musical by bringing a few people together during difficulty provided solace for the souls of an entire nation seventy-five years later.

Walking alone makes the burdens heavier and the victories emptier.

We need one another. Walking alone isn't optional.

I get to pastor a church that models community: Life groups. One-on-one mentoring at coffee shops. Men and women and students gathering around tables to learn from each other. People completing odd jobs at the homes of the elderly and single moms. Prayer drive-throughs and food giveaways. Help with home disasters like fires and floods. Assistance for adults with intellectual disabilities. Compassion outreaches. Help with rent and other vital needs. Ministry to families of the incarcerated—things that are the essence of Christlike community.

From the very beginning, we were created to walk with others. God Himself said, *"It is not good for the man to be alone"* (Genesis 2:18, NLT). This truth speaks to the built-in need our souls have for belonging.

Life is filled with both joys and struggles. Walking alone makes the burdens heavier and the victories emptier. When we go through pain, grief, or loss, having others to lean on brings strength and hope. When we celebrate, having others to share our joy makes it all the richer.

---

59 Laura Snapes "Captain Tom Moore becomes oldest artist to claim UK No 1 single," *The Guardian,* 24 Apr. 2020, https://www.theguardian.com/music/2020/apr/24/captain-tom-moore-becomes-oldest-artist-to-claim-uk-no-1-single.

In 1927, Charles Lindbergh became the first person to fly solo nonstop across the Atlantic, piloting The Spirit of St. Louis from New York to Paris. It was one of the great achievements of the 20th century—a feat of courage, endurance, and skill. Those thirty-three grueling hours in the air were spent completely alone, with no one to share the thrill of the flight. After hours of pushing the limits of human endurance, battling exhaustion and isolation, he landed to a massive crowd of 150,000 strangers who had gathered to welcome him—alone in a crowd.[60]

Neil Armstrong walked down the steps of *Apollo 11* to plant his feet on the moon to the audible cheers of no one but himself.

Howard Hughes, once one of the richest people in the world, spent his final years as a recluse, hidden away in hotel rooms with no one around him.

Michael Jackson lived a life of immense fame, but ended his life surrounded by bodyguards instead of true friends.

Even with wealth and fame, loneliness can still creep in. We need people to celebrate and walk through life with.

When you can't stand by yourself, true friends will stand alongside you.

Real friendship means carrying each other—sometimes literally.

Rick Hoyt was born with cerebral palsy and was unable to walk or speak. His father, Dick Hoyt, dedicated his life to making sure Rick experienced as full and meaningful a

---

60 "New York-to-Paris Flight." *Charles Lindbergh House and Museum.* Accessed June 19, 2025. https://www.mnhs.org/lindbergh/learn/aviation/famous-flight.

life as anyone. Together they participated in over a thousand races, including marathons and triathlons, with Dick pushing Rick in a wheelchair every step of the way. Their bond went beyond father and son—they were friends displaying unconditional love, personal sacrifice, and unwavering support.[61]

The Bible repeatedly reinforces that we matter to each other.

"Two are better than one, because they have a good return for their labor: If either of them falls down, one can help the other up. But pity anyone who falls and has no one to help them up" (Ecclesiastes 4:9-10).

"Carry each other's burdens, and in this way you will fulfill the law of Christ" (Galatians 6:2).

David and Jonathan, Ruth and Naomi, Jesus and Mary, Martha and Lazarus—all friends who stood with one another.

In the New Testament, Jesus did not walk His earthly journey alone. He surrounded Himself with disciples who became His friends, even more poignantly with three of His disciples. In some of His most challenging human moments—in a sea-swept boat, in ministry, in Gethsemane—He had people with Him.

The early Church is described in the Book of Acts as a community living in fellowship, sharing resources, praying together, and bearing each other's burdens (Acts 2:42-47).

---

61 "Dick Hoyt—A Father's Story, Part III." *MyChild at CerebalPalsy.org.* Accessed June 19, 2025. https://www.cerebralpalsy.org/inspiration/athletes/dick-hoyt/fathers-story-part-iii.

If the Son of God and the early Church understood the power of having friends to lock arms with, how much more do we need community in the world we live in today?

Faith is strongest when it is shared.

One of the greatest spiritual revivals happening today is in Communist China. Despite widespread persecution, underground churches are thriving. Believers have lost their jobs, homes, and freedom for practicing faith.

The gospel multiplies despite persecution. Christians gather in secret, risking their lives to worship, pray, and read Scripture together. When one believer is arrested, another takes his place in leadership. When Bibles are scarce, they memorize scripture to pass it along orally. This strength comes not merely from resilience, but by the power of faith shared in community.

IIIIIIIIIIIIIIIIIIIIIIIIIIIIIIIIIIIIIIIIIIIIIIIIIIIIIIIIIIIIIIIIIIIIIIIIIIIIIIIIIIIII

Faith is strongest when it is shared.

IIIIIIIIIIIIIIIIIIIIIIIIIIIIIIIIIIIIIIIIIIIIIIIIIIIIIIIIIIIIIIIIIIIIIIIIIIIIIIIIIIIII

Years ago, I visited Shenzhen, China. I was with two friends, and we were staying in a hotel I can only describe as institutional. The Four Seasons it was not. We had been warned that very likely the rooms were bugged, and we needed to be careful about who and what we talked about.

This did not encourage a good night's sleep. I talk in my sleep sometimes, and I was terrified I would say something illegal in between snores.

The next morning, having woken still a free man, I showered under a spigot whose meager water pressure and chilly temperature encouraged a fast washing. Especially since there was no soap.

After dressing, I was informed that we were expecting a visitor—a man who had just been released from a Chinese prison the day before, after spending thirty-five years behind bars. I wondered what he had been in prison for, so I asked our host. Turns out he was arrested and convicted for sharing his faith about Jesus.

Okay. And he's coming here? To my room? In fifteen minutes? Should we check for listening devices behind the curtains, under the bed, in the lamp shades, the sprinklers? It was an unsettling moment.

It so happened that the man was fifty years old when he was taken into custody—that made him eighty-five years old now. He came into the room bowed over, no more than seventy-five pounds, a wizened face exposing his trials, and with a visage I'll never forget—a huge smile on his face still showing all thirty-two teeth. He proceeded to testify through a translator, his story of sharing Jesus with people before his arrest and the thirty-five years he spent in prison doing the same—according to him, because "Jesus is Lord."

I don't recall that he ever shared his name—perhaps that was on purpose—but today, the church in China is not looking back. It thrives because of the unbreakable and tested faith of people like Mr. X and a body of faith-filled believers.

Faith is strongest when it is shared.

The journey of the soul is indisputably communal, but we must be willing to press pause in order to enjoy the fruit of it. Our souls need the kind of encouragement and faith-building that only connecting with other souls can bring.

The Almighty Mirror

My family loves games. Board games. Word games. Charades. Twister. If it involves dice, cards, or spinners, we're in. It's a staple of any Taylor family gathering. On one occasion, I remember a game that asked each of us to match certain qualities with the people around the circle. It was entertaining and revealing—and now and then it forced vulnerability to the surface—the kind of awesome game that has the capacity to bust up families.

One of the questions asked: "Name the person who would most likely look twice as they walked past a mirror." I could think of more than one Taylor that might apply to. When we turned over the cards one-by-one to reveal each person's answer, the name that was in the majority was mine. So my clan believes that of all the people in our tribe, I am the person most likely to exemplify vanity. Truth be told, they aren't wrong. And they know it. I am a fan of the mirror, though hopefully not to the level of mythical Narcissus.

A mirror, at its core, reflects what stands in front of it. It captures both the beauty and flaws of its subject. A community does the same; it reflects those who shape it—their values, their struggles, their dreams, their grit and spirit.

A mirror can't reflect something that doesn't present itself. A community is the sum of its people's actions, relationships, values, and attitudes.

A compassionate community reflects kindness and unity. It represents people lifting one another, working toward a common good that is beyond any one individual. A selfish community reflects pride and materialism. It is fractured by division and injustice. Both are mirrors, one divulging wounds and challenges, the other revealing joys and pure motives.

The mirror also reminds us that change is possible. When we see our reflection, we adjust our posture, fix our hair, rearrange our clothes, modify our expression. Communities do, too. If it doesn't like the reflection it sees, it has the power to change. The people within can choose to build something better, something stronger.

One of the best things about a mirror is that it never judges. You and I do, but a mirror? Never. Not once as I've passed by the sheet glass window of a downtown Chicago Miracle Mile store—the quintessential look-three-times mirror—has it ever chastised me or told me anything new— it simply reflects the unvarnished truth.

So does the community. It reflects whatever walks its own streets. When we pause to look at the community we are part of, what do we see?

Ubuntu

One of the greatest honors of my life was being chosen by the college I attended to represent my school for the summer just prior to my senior year as a missions ambassador to South Africa. I was only nineteen at the time, and the assignment took me all the way to Cape Town, situated at the bottom of the African continent.

It is, without exaggeration or bias, one of the most stunning places on earth. The natural beauty of the city is not just a backdrop—it is part of the soul of the city. From Table Mountain to the sandy beaches, the deep blue waters off the coast where the Indian and Atlantic Oceans meet, the red rooftops, and the lush hills that roll right down to the water, it is a place that feels as if the world has paused in perfect harmony.

And yet, when I arrived that year, harmony was a faraway dream. Apartheid was in full swing. Apartheid was a system of racial segregation and discrimination in South Africa that lasted from the 1940s to the early 1990s. The term is Afrikaans for "separateness."

During that period, non-White South Africans were forced to live separately from Whites and used different public facilities. Most lived in sub-standard housing. Years of violent protests by Black South Africans led to a weakening of support for apartheid. The movement was led by Nelson Mandela, who endured twenty-seven years in a South African prison. His social work resulted in the official end of apartheid, though real struggles there continue widely.

"The word is perhaps now better known as an award winning computer desktop and operating system, but the term originated in South Africa, emphasizing community connectedness and compassion. The word itself means *"I am because we are,"* meaning that a person's identity and well-being are strongly tied to the community around them. Ubuntu was not just a word—it described a way of life that shaped cultures all across Africa and inspired movements around the world. It taught that true strength came from cooperation, empathy, and the idea that one's success is linked to the success of others in the community.[62]

Ubuntu was seen practiced in everyday African life. In many villages, neighbors looked after each other's children, families shared food, elders passed on wisdom to younger generations. An individual's well-being was the community's responsibility.

Our lives impact those around us. Small acts of kindness—helping a friend, sharing knowledge, showing compassion—are all ways we can continue living Ubuntu. In a world that often emphasizes individualism, this philosophy reminds us that we are at our best when we lift each other.

Pausing to value community is essential. It also comes with inherent challenges. Conflicts, misunderstandings, and disappointments are inevitable whenever people come together. The philosophy of Ubuntu encourages grace and forgiveness, sensitivity and mercy. It teaches patience,

---

62 "Ubuntu philosophy," *Wikipedia,* last modified May 23, 2025, accessed June 19, 2025, https://en.wikipedia.org/wiki/Ubuntu_philosophy#:~:text=Ubuntu%20(Zulu%20pronunciation%3A%20%5B%C3%B9%C9%93%C3%BAnt%CA%BC%C3%B9,surrounding%20societal%20and%20physical%20worlds.

resilience, and the importance of reconciliation, all of which are vital to the soul that desires more of God.

Pausing to be in community with others is not a peripheral aspect of spiritual soul care; it is central to it.

One Another

It might be easy to understand why we should pause to Sabbath or listen to or abide in Jesus, but pausing to consider the value of community is not automatically seen as vitally linked to soul enrichment. But it is.

In the Bible, many scriptures speak to our relationship with "one another"—gospel things that can only be fulfilled in the company of someone else. These passages place a premium on the value of making space to elevate community as a priority.

Take them one by one below. See how many characterize your walk with Christ and with others.

On a scale of 1 (not so much) to 10 (off the charts!), where do you place yourself with regard to each?

Accept One Another: *"Accept one another, then, just as Christ accepted you, in order to bring praise to God"* (Romans 15:7)

1   2   3   4   5   6   7   8   9   1 0

Agree With One Another: *"Agree with one another, live in peace; and the God of love and peace will be with you"* (2 Corinthians 13:11, ESV).

1   2   3   4   5   6   7   8   9   1 0

Be at Peace With One Another: *"Have salt in yourselves, and be at peace with each other"* (Mark 9:50).

1   2   3   4   5   6   7   8   9   1 0

Be Humble Toward One Another: *"All of you, clothe yourselves with humility toward one another, because, 'God opposes the proud but shows favor to the humble'"* (1 Peter 5:5).

1   2   3   4   5   6   7   8   9   1 0

Be Kind to One Another: *"Be kind to one another, tenderhearted"* (Ephesians 4:32, ESV).

1   2   3   4   5   6   7   8   9   1 0

Bear One Another's Burdens: *"Bear one another's burdens, and so fulfill the law of Christ"* (Galatians 6:2, ESV).

1   2   3   4   5   6   7   8   9   1 0

Bear With One Another: *"With all humility and gentleness, with patience, bearing with one another in love, eager to maintain the unity of the Spirit in the bond of peace"* (Ephesians 4:2-3, ESV).

1   2   3   4   5   6   7   8   9   1 0

Build One Another Up: *"Build one another up, just as you are doing"* (1 Thessalonians 5:11, ESV).

1   2   3   4   5   6   7   8   9   1 0

Care for One Another: *"That there may be no division in the body, but that the members may have the same care for one another"* (1 Corinthians 12:25, ESV).

1   2   3   4   5   6   7   8   9   1 0

Comfort One Another: *"Brothers, rejoice. Aim for restoration, comfort one another"* (2 Corinthians 13:11, ESV).

1   2   3   4   5   6   7   8   9   1 0

Confess Sins to One Another: *"Confess your sins to one another"* (James 5:16, ESV).

1   2   3   4   5   6   7   8   9   1 0

Do Good to One Another: *"See that no one repays anyone evil for evil, but always seek to do good to one another and to everyone"* (1 Thessalonians 5:15, ESV).

1   2   3   4   5   6   7   8   9   1 0

Encourage One Another: *"Not neglecting to meet together, as is the habit of some, but encouraging one another, and all the more as you see the Day drawing near"* (Hebrews 10:25, ESV).

1   2   3   4   5   6   7   8   9   1 0

Exhort One Another: *"Exhort one another every day, as long as it is called 'today,' that none of you may be hardened by the deceitfulness of sin"* (Hebrews 3:13, ESV).

1   2   3   4   5   6   7   8   9   1 0

Greet One Another: *"Greet one another with the kiss of love. Peace to all of you who are in Christ"* (1 Peter 5:14).

1   2   3   4   5   6   7   8   9   1 0

Have Fellowship With One Another: *"But if we walk in the light, as he is in the light, we have fellowship with one another, and the blood of Jesus his Son cleanses us from all sin"* (1 John 1:7, ESV).

1   2   3   4   5   6   7   8   9   1 0

Honor One Another: *"Outdo one another in showing honor"* (Romans 12:10, ESV).

1   2   3   4   5   6   7   8   9   1 0

Instruct One Another: *"I myself am satisfied about you, my brothers, that you yourselves are full of goodness, filled with all knowledge and able to instruct one another"* (Romans 15:14, ESV).

1   2   3   4   5   6   7   8   9   1 0

Live in Harmony With One Another: *"Live in harmony with one another. Do not be haughty, but associate with the lowly. Never be wise in your own sight"* (Romans 12:16, ESV).

1   2   3   4   5   6   7   8   9   1 0

Love One Another: *"This is my commandment, that you love one another as I have loved you"* (John 15:12, ESV).

1   2   3   4   5   6   7   8   9   1 0

Pray for One Another: *"Pray for one another, that you may be healed. The prayer of a righteous person has great power as it is working"* (James 5:16, ESV).

1   2   3   4   5   6   7   8   9   10

Serve One Another: *"For you were called to freedom, brothers. Only do not use your freedom as an opportunity for the flesh, but through love serve one another"* (Galatians 5:13, ESV).

1   2   3   4   5   6   7   8   9   10

Show Hospitality to One Another: *"Show hospitality to one another without grumbling"* (1 Peter 4:9, ESV).

1   2   3   4   5   6   7   8   9   10

Sing With One Another: *"Addressing one another in psalms and hymns and spiritual songs, singing and making melody to the Lord with your heart"* (Ephesians 5:19, ESV).

1   2   3   4   5   6   7   8   9   10

Stir One Another: *"Let us consider how to stir one another to love and good works"* (Hebrews 10:24, ESV).

1   2   3   4   5   6   7   8   9   10

Submit to One Another: *"Submitting to one another out of reverence for Christ"* (Ephesians 5:21, ESV).

1   2   3   4   5   6   7   8   9   10

Teach and Admonish One Another: *"Let the word of Christ dwell in you richly, teaching and admonishing one another in all wisdom, singing psalms and hymns and spiritual songs, with thankfulness in your hearts to God* (Colossians 3:16, ESV).

1   2   3   4   5   6   7   8   9   1 0

How did you do? Where is there room for personal growth and "others" care? Pausing to prioritize one another by living out the value of community is how our souls come to health.

Doing Life

Joelene and I have spent many years in close-knit community with others—doing life with people both "old" and "young." For years, we were in a life group with couples twenty years our junior. That time was precious to us. We were a spiritual father and mother to those couples—we became genuine friends despite the gap in our ages. It was a beautiful time of saturating ourselves with the gospel together while eating chips and salsa. After nearly a decade with that group, we decided it was time for a change. As tremendous as those years had been, we were ready for a community closer to our own ages, where we could share similar life experiences, joys, struggles, pains, and celebrations.

We landed in a group with folks who immediately "got us." People in our stage of life who didn't call us by our pastoral titles—we were just Kevin and Joelene. That community made us feel seen and understood. There was little need to overly monitor ourselves or explain our words. They just knew. The laughter we shared was soul medicine. Sharing the hard stuff was soul therapy. For years, we looked forward to connecting every week to study the Bible, eat, pray, serve our community, and do life together.

There's nothing like friends cheering you on to make the win bigger. Better. Sweeter. That same community can also call you out when you need to be held accountable for words, actions, responses, and habits that have pulled you off course. They remind you of the person you know you're supposed to be.

All of that is love—and love is at the center of the "one anothers"—and that is breath and life to your soul. But you don't get it by rushing through. You must decide to press pause to possess it.

Parable of the Oak

The small village of Flourish, tucked between rolling hills and the sea, was a community unlike any other. It wasn't famous, nor was it particularly rich. It didn't have towering buildings or fancy monuments. What it had was something far more valuable.

At the heart of the village was an old oak tree, massive and wise, its roots stretching outward underground to reach beneath the town square. People gathered under the giant tree every day—to chat, to sip coffee, to people watch, to hang out.

Mr. Hayden, the town baker, had a shop on the northeast corner of the square. Every morning he woke before the sun, kneading dough, because he loved the way people lit up when they took their first bite of his freshly baked goods. He was known to say, "Food tastes better when shared," as he passed warm bread to whoever stopped by, his trademark act of congeniality and generosity.

On the other end of the square, opposite the baker, was Mr. Jenson's place, the old carpenter. His specialty was handmade wooden toys, but he never charged the children for the miniatures he made. His motto was, "Laughter is payment enough," and people always wondered how the carpenter could stay in business. Mr. Jenson had never married and had once been such a lonely man, but the village had not let him stay that way. They checked in on him and made sure he always had company.

The widow who lived on the edge of town had lost her husband the year before, and yet she found herself surrounded by the villagers. Meals appeared mysteriously at her door. Gifts were dropped off now and then. Money showed up in her mailbox. Though she was burdened with grief, she learned to smile again because Flourish didn't leave her to carry it alone.

When someone fell ill, the village cared for them. When someone had good news, the village celebrated with them. And when someone felt lost, the village reminded them they belonged.

One day, a traveler passing through asked the town elder, "What makes this place so special? There are no riches here, no great wonders."

The elder simply smiled and pointed at the oak tree where people were gathered, laughing, sharing stories, and encouraging one another. "This," he said, " is the greatest treasure of all."

So the village of Flourish thrived—not because of what it had, but because of *who* it had.

Who do *you* have? And who has *you?*

A Prayer for Community

Heavenly Father,
Thank You for creating us to walk in community, just as
You exist in perfect unity—Father, Son, and Holy Spirit. You
have called us not to walk alone, but to bear one another's
burdens, encourage one another, and grow together in faith.
Lord, help us to love as You love—to build relationships
that reflect Your grace and truth. May we be a people who
uplift the weak and stand firm in trials together. Teach us
to serve, forgive, and speak life into each other's souls.
Bind us together as one body in Christ, united in purpose
and love. Let our communities be places of healing, strength,
and discipleship, where Your presence is made known. May
we never take for granted the gift of fellowship, and may we
always seek to glorify You in the way we love one another.
Amen.

PAUSE HACK: Stretch and breathe deeply. Even a two-minute stretch or deep breathing session can set the tone for the day.

||||||||||||||||||||||||||||||||||||||||||||||||||||||||||||||||||||

1-Hour Soul Pause Application: Community

It's okay if you're unable to complete the entire practice in one sitting. Give yourself permission to move at a pace that's gentle and sustainable—soul care isn't a race, but a journey of presence and grace.

To embrace the beauty and import of soul care, find a quiet and private place where you can be fully present with Jesus.

Things to have with you:
» A Bible (paper or digital)
» Notebook paper to write on
» Something to write with

You are encouraged to write in your book. By dedicating this hour to soul care, you align your heart with God's peace and presence.

Minutes 1-10: Begin

Take the first ten minutes and invite God's presence into this time of soul care. Pray for an open heart and mind to receive from God.

Learn to sit with Jesus in the room. Take some deep breaths and reflect on His love for you.

Minutes 10-25: Scripture and Self-Reflection

Read the passages below.

1) **Love One Another**—John 13:34-35
2) **Encourage One Another**—1 Thessalonians 5:11
3) **Forgive One Another**—Colossians 3:13
4) **Bear One Another's Burdens**—Galatians 6:2
5) **Serve One Another**—Galatians 5:13
6) **Pray for One Another**—James 5:16

Take time to assess your heart in light of the above commands. On a scale from 1 to 5, how do you feel you are living out each one?

LOVING OTHERS

(not so well)   (really well)

1	2	3	4	5

ENCOURAGING OTHERS

(not so well)   (really well)

1	2	3	4	5

FORGIVING OTHERS

(not so well)   (really well)

1	2	3	4	5

BEARING WITH OTHERS

(not so well)   (really well)

1	2	3	4	5

SERVING OTHERS
(not so well)   (really well)

1   2   3   4   5

PRAYING FOR OTHERS
(not so well)   (really well)

1   2   3   4   5

Below each value above is a blank line. Who is God speaking to you about:
- » Loving better?
- » Encouraging more?
- » Forgiving?
- » Bearing with?
- » Serving more?
- » Praying for?

Write their names on the line below the scale.

Now ask God for open doors to love, encourage, forgive, bear with, serve and pray. Determine to reach out to them this week.

Minutes 25-45: Others Reflection
Think now about whether you've been on the receiving end of each of the above "one another" values. Who has ministered to you? Write their names on the blanks below.

Who has loved you? _____

Who has encouraged you? _____

Who has forgiven you? _____

Who has borne with you? _____

Who has served you? _____

Who has prayed for you? _____

With the paper you brought along, select one of those people and write a letter of thanks and encouragement to bless them. Send a text or email this week.

Minutes 45-55: Prayer

- » Pray for strength to live out the "one another" commands.
- » Lift up specific relationships or burdens.
- » Pray for God's love to deepen within the community you're part of.

Minutes 55-60: Blessing

Close with gratitude, thanking God for His presence and the people He has placed in your life.

"May the Lord make you increase and abound in love for one another and for all, as we do for you (1 Thessalonians 3:12, ESV).

"Beloved, I pray that all may go well with you and that you may be in good health, as it goes well with your soul."

—3 John 2 (ESV)

Song:

"FRIENDSHIP WITH JESUS"
by Joseph C. Ludgate (1898)[63]

---

63 Joseph C. Ludgate, "Friendship With Jesus," 1898, public domain.

Chapter 11

Happy Trails to You

"This is a wonderful day. I've never seen this one before."
—Attributed to Maya Angelou

I don't know that I'm a naturally outdoorsy kind of person. You know, the kind who really craves fresh air (not that I prefer stale air), walks in the woods, and basks in the sun like a cat on a windowsill.

Let's just say my connection with the outdoors is ... complicated. Take mountain hiking, for instance. This type of hiking typically turns into what I'll call "walking in its most unwelcome form." What begins as a nice, pleasant stroll quickly turns into an uphill battle against gravity with sweat pouring from every pore until it dawns on me that for the last four weeks I should have been doing cardio every day instead of binge-watching Netflix.

Camelback Mountain just outside Phoenix is one of the premier climbing opportunities and tourist stops in Arizona. The Echo Canyon Trail is rated as "extremely difficult." It is described as a "strenuous" climb, featuring exposed rock with "sections of hand-over-hand climbing."[64]

Wow. Sounds fun. Dogs are prohibited. If they won't even let dogs on the trail, well ...

This is the kind of hiking that causes you to seriously question your life choices.

The beginning section of our "trail" lulled us into a false sense of confidence—a few pleasant switchbacks at first, a nice dirt path. Then suddenly we were faced with a nearly vertical climb where our only assistant was a rail by which to hoist ourselves up. Meanwhile, athletic people forty years our junior were scaling the rocks all around us like ibex while we clung to the rail—praying for Jesus to come— or at least that our arms didn't give out. I never had such respect for gravity. When Joelene and I climbed Camelback, I seriously considered faking an injury just so I could sit down for a while.

That said, we both made it to the top. I won't share how long it took us, but I didn't have a beard when we started. The true reward, though, is the incredible vista that can only be seen from the top—a panoramic view and, to be honest, worth the struggle.

---

64 "Camelback Mountain," *Visit Pheonix,* accessed June 19, 2025, https://www.visitphoenix.com/sonoran-desert/parks/camelback-mountain/.

Reaching the top of a mountain is an experience that's hard to put into words. It's an accomplishment. Even with other journeyers, making it to the top (which automatically puts you on this winning team with complete strangers) there's a built-in solitude that pervades the moment. You can be alone in a crowd there. Every step to get to the summit, every bit of effort and expended breath, makes the moment feel earned. When you're at last standing there, the whole world seems to stretch out below you—everything feels a bit smaller and even simpler. You aren't thinking about schedules or stress or noise. You're just there—and *there* is all that matters—fully present.

You sit for a while to catch your breath, but after your blood pressure has come back to *Homo sapiens* levels, you're taking it all in—the vastness of it. You don't want to leave. Clarity and perspective about life become sharper.

After a respectable amount of time at the top of Camelback, watching other climbers raise their hands in victory as they broke the top of the hill, it was time to descend. I can't say the way down was easier. I felt muscles in my legs I didn't know were there, and the steep decline is a mix of triumph and terror. But Camelback Mountain is a rite of passage. We made it. Up and down. We did it. Nature did not get the best of us. It embraced us.

There is something profoundly healing about pausing to step outside and immerse yourself in nature for soul health. Studies have shown that time spent in nature reduces stress hormones, lowers blood pressure, and improves mental well-being. Beyond the physical and psychological benefits, nature offers a spiritual dimension that is overlooked and underestimated.

Throughout history, seekers of wisdom—monks, poets, prophets—have retreated to nature to encounter something—Someone—greater than themselves. That something—that Someone—is the reason mountain peaks, desert landscapes, and rivers have coaxed humanity to meet the Divine in meeting places that, over time, became sacred.

» Mount Fuji in Japan is a spiritual site in Shinto and Buddhist traditions.

» Mount Sinai is revered in Judaism, Christianity, and Islam as the place where Moses received the Commandments.

» Mount Olympus in Greece is considered the home of mythological gods.

» The Sahara Desert in North Africa is sacred to many Islamic groups.

» The Judean Desert in Israel is important in Christian and Jewish faiths.

» The Thar Desert in India and Pakistan is home to Hindu temples and Sufi shrines.

» The Ganges River is one of the holiest bodies of water in Hinduism.

» The Nile River is worshiped by Egyptians as a source of life and blessing and is a key landmark in Old Testament teaching.

» The Indus River in India is integral to Hindu and Buddhist traditions.

Nature is celebrated throughout the Bible. Beyond page one, we find nature and creation composing its own worship song: *"The mountains and the hills before you shall break forth into singing, and all the trees of the field shall clap their hands"* (Isaiah 55:12, ESV).

Psalm 148 calls on the sun, moon, stars, mountains, and animals to praise God.

Luke 19 exclaims that the rocks will cry out in praise to God if we fail to.

Jesus points to birds and flowers as examples of His care for us, illustrating that if He provides for them, surely He provides for us. (Matthew 6:26-30)

Jesus taught in parables and stories with examples from nature:

» The Mustard Seed (Matthew 13)—He uses a tiny seed to illustrate the growth of God's Kingdom.

» The Vine and Branches (John 15)—He compares our relationship with Him to limbs connected to a source.

» The Sower and the Soils (Matthew 13)—He teaches a lesson of spiritual growth using the imagery of agriculture.

The big outdoors serves as a revelation for the character of God. Psalm 19:1 says, *"The heavens declare the glory of God; the skies proclaim the work of His hands."*

No matter your faith or religion, everyone seems to understand there is something healing about stepping outside and immersing yourself in God's handiwork. You may never verbalize that, but you feel it. The world of nature has an innate and unique ability to beckon us to pause, slow down, and escape the press of life.

"In the beginning God created the heavens and the earth" (Genesis 1:1).

God made it all. Expand it beyond the planets and stars we can see with the naked eye to galaxies, solar systems, interstellar space, every black hole and asteroid, nebula and neutron star, the cosmic web—I don't even know what that is; I read it somewhere—but I guarantee, if it's out there, God made it. Everything designed with a purpose and an intention.

Walk outside and turn your eyes upward. A world of beauty unfolds.

By day, the expanse of sky stretches endlessly, painted in varying shades of blue. The sun casts a golden light, filtering through soft clouds or by glowing rays that burst through the gaps with dramatic beams. Birds glide effortlessly, their wings elongated as they dance on unseen currents. The leaves of towering trees sway gently, their branches reaching toward the sky like outstretched arms.

At dusk, the sky is transformed into a masterpiece of color—fiery oranges and pinks melting into deep purples and indigos. The crescent moon hangs in the twilight, watching over everything below like a noiseless sentinel.

When darkness finally settles, the night sky unveils its most breathtaking wonders of all. Stars burn brilliantly, scattered across infinite sky. If you're lucky, you might glimpse a shooting star streaking across the heavens or see the northern lights dance in waves of green, blue, and violet.

The world God created is, in a word, breathtaking.

|||||||||||||||||||||||||||||||||||||||||||||||||||||||||||||||||||||||||||||||||||||||||||

There's just something about nature that demands we press pause.

|||||||||||||||||||||||||||||||||||||||||||||||||||||||||||||||||||||||||||||||||||||||||||

Zion National Park in Utah has been recognized as an International Dark Sky location. It is a place where the night sky is protected from artificial light—light pollution—so the view of the stars is not inhibited and nocturnal wildlife is not disturbed.[65]

We had the privilege of visiting Zion a few years ago—you know... to hike. Due to its remote location and high canyon walls, Zion offers incredible night views of the Milky Way and constellations. When the sun set, we drove into the area to experience what "true dark" looks and feels like. You could barely see your hand in front of your face. We found a place to pull over, got out of the car, and lay on our backs on the hood like Danny Zuko and Sandy in *Grease*,[66] gazing at the splendor of those celestial bodies.

Looking up reminded us how small we are in the grand design of it all. It filled us with awe and a deep connection to Someone beyond us.

65 "Lighting Project Protects Zion's Starry Night Sky," *National Park Service,* accessed June 19, 2025, https://www.nps.gov/zion/learn/nature/night_friendly_lighting.htm.
66 Randal Kleiser, *Grease* (June 16, 1978; Hollywood, CA: Paramount Pictures).

There's just something about nature that demands we press pause.

There's Just Something About...

There's just something about the ocean.

Some years ago, we had the opportunity to visit the Maldives. We flew into Malé, the capital, and then took a boat for an hour and a half to one of the islands.

Once we got beyond the port toward open water, the boat that took us to our destination encountered rougher seas. It began to lurch violently as towering waves crashed over us, sending Poseidon-like sheets of saltwater spraying into the air, churning with Herculean force beneath us. Each wave lifted the boat and its passengers into the air before dropping us down onto what felt like concrete with a stomach-twisting plunge. Our hands squeezed the seat in front of us with a death-grip and our knuckles turned white with each heart-pounding sway. A wave tipped the boat at an alarming angle. For terrifying minutes, it felt as if the sea might swallow us whole. It was the closest I've come to feeling "this might be it." I was praying the boat would hold together long enough to reach shore.

The ocean is vast and ever-changing. Every time I stand before it, I am confronted with something that invites me and humbles me all at once. Maybe it is the sheer enormity of it that puts things in perspective.

And then there is the sound—that continuous and thunderous roar. The magnificent volume of water crashing over the edge of Niagara Falls at three thousand tons per second creates an omnipotent, rumbling vibration that I can feel in my chest—a natural symphony of raw power.

The tides remind me that life is cyclical. They testify that life moves in rhythms, pulling me forward and backward, never fully within my control. It is calm one moment and raging the next—a place of both serenity and danger, a sanctuary as well as a force to be reckoned with. Standing at its edge I never feel as insignificant as in that moment.

There's just something about the ocean.

||||||||||||||||||||||||||||||||||||||||||||||||||||||||||||||||||||||

There's just something about the mountains.

Earth's ancient sentinels—silent and strong, unshakeable. Perhaps it is their stillness that attracts me. They are untouched by the hurry of life. They remind me that not everything is urgent, that there is wisdom in patience. When I stand before them, there is a sense that time is slow and steady, unfazed by my hastiness.

Mountains are sacred. Throughout history, they have been places of divine encounter. Their elevation alone makes me feel closer to God, almost as if I could touch the sky from there.

One of our most memorable trips was to Nepal, high in the Himalayas. To stand on the peaks above is like being on the edge of the world, where earth meets sky. The air is razor-thin, each breath a noticeable struggle as icy winds slice through clothing and bite at skin.

The view is unlike anything seen before. Jagged peaks with snow-capped summits stretch as far as the eye can see. The silence is profound. The rest of the world seems unimportant compared to the grandeur of one of nature's great masterpieces.

Mountains are not merely admired from a distance; they demand to be scaled and conquered. They call out to those who seek life beyond the ordinary. The journey up is never easy and yet, reaching the peak brings a perspective that can't be found anywhere at sea level. From "up there," life takes a new view—the struggles and noise and worries "down there" shrink by comparison.

There's just something about the mountains.

||||||||||||||||||||||||||||||||||||||||||||||||||||||||||||||||||

There's just something about the forest.

Bavaria, in southern Germany, is a favorite place of ours. It is a land filled with storybook villages, green meadows, and crystal clear lakes. In the countryside, timbered houses with flower-filled balconies dot the hills, their red-tiled roofs standing out against the lush green. Church steeples rise above quaint villages, their bells tolling on the hour throughout the valleys. It is a land of fairy tales come to life, not the least of which is the magical Black Forest.

We have driven through this enchanting alpine region many times and it never fails to leave a lasting imprint. It is a world to itself—alive, breathing, old as the hills. Time seems to slow there. To step into the forest is to step away from the rest of the world. It calls us to wander—and wonder. After all, Little Red Riding Hood, Hansel and Gretel, and Rapunzel all live in the forest.

Maybe it's the sense of mystery found here. This is where I have heard my own thoughts more than anywhere else in creation. Distractions are stripped away. The trees do not strive—they simply are—deeply rooted and reaching higher than the year before. With impenetrable trunks, they seem to be bearers of wisdom and examples of endurance.

The forest's silence does not mean it does not speak. It is rich with stories—stories as ancient as the trees themselves—etched into the gnarled bark of old oaks. The forest is a living book, and it seems that every time I enter, I become part of its tale.

There's just something about the forest.

|||||||||||||||||||||||||||||||||||||||||||||||||||||||||||||||||||||||||

There's just something about the desert.

Compared to the others, it is a place of extremes—vast, barren, seemingly lifeless, yet alive in ways not immediately seen. It is a place of survival and deep spiritual meaning. The desert strips everything down to bare minimums. It offers no easy comforts—only open spaces and relentless sun. In the vast stillness, you are left alone with yourself— both unsettling and enlightening.

Life here is not abundant, but what does survive is strong. The cactus conserves its water; creatures move by night to avoid the heat; the wind carves rock and sand over centuries. The desert reminds us that scarcity is not the same as emptiness—that even in the harshest places, life finds a way.

|||||||||||||||||||||||||||||||||||||||||||||||||||||||||||||||||||||||||||||||||||||||||

Sometimes the most unexpected beauty comes not from what is present, but from what is absent.

|||||||||||||||||||||||||||||||||||||||||||||||||||||||||||||||||||||||||||||||||||||||||

During our visit to the dunes outside of Dubai, we roamed across mountains of sand in a Land Cruiser. Its massive tires dug into the soft, golden sand, kicking up clouds of dust behind us. We climbed towering dunes as tall as mountains before cresting the peak—that brief moment of weightlessness—and then plunging down the other side with heart-racing descent.

The desert has long been a place of spiritual seeking. Prophets, mystics, and nomads have retreated into its wilderness, searching for clarity, for revelation, for God. Moses encountered the burning bush in the desert, Jesus fasted there for forty days in solitude, John the Baptist prepared the people for the Messiah there, Elijah and David fled there to escape danger. Countless others have stepped into its vastness to quiet the noise and hear something deeper.

It is not without beauty—perhaps not to be compared to the lush gardens of the forest or snow-capped mountains—but beautiful in its rawness and vacantness. It is a reminder to me that sometimes the most unexpected beauty comes not from what is present, but from what is absent.

There's just something about the desert.

IIIIIIIIIIIIIIIIIIIIIIIIIIIIIIIIIIIIIIIIIIIIIIIIIIIIIIIIIIIIIIIIIIII

There's just something about the seasons.

The seasons are more than just shifts in weather—they are the flow of life itself. They remind us that everything moves in cycles of growth, decline, and renewal.

Maybe it is their inevitability. No matter what we do, we cannot stop or slow the changing of the guard. Winter will follow autumn, spring will break through the frost, summer's warmth will return again. The seasons are a reminder that time waits for no one, that change is as natural as the air we breathe. Like them all or not, we learn to live with them—to adapt, to embrace, to find joy in each passing phase.

The seasons carry symbolism. Spring is the season of beginnings, of fresh possibilities, of things coming to life. It is a reminder that after every hardship, there is renewal. Summer bursts forth in full bloom, a time of energy, movement, and long, warm days. Then comes autumn, the season of transformation, of letting go, of learning to find beauty in endings. And finally winter—a time of reflection and waiting.

The seasons mirror my own life—my youth, my passions, my moments of loss, and my times of rest and excitement. No season lasts forever, no matter how much I wish it. The heat of summer fades, the barrenness of winter softens. Just as with life, the hardest times do not stay forever, but neither do the easiest. The seasons teach me that endings make way for beginnings, and that every stage has its purpose.

There's just something about the seasons.

||||||||||||||||||||||||||||||||||||||||||||||||||||||||||||||||||||||

Nature is the one place that reinforces soul care in ways that words cannot. It is the one setting where you can fully engage and yet say nothing at all and still be refreshed and healed. The natural world is not affected by your urgent to-do list. Trees do not rush to grow, and the sun does not hurry its rising. Nature shifts our focus from productivity to presence, from striving to abiding, from doing to being.

||||||||||||||||||||||||||||||||||||||||||||||||||||||||||||||||||||||||

It isn't just the presence of nature that restores; it is the determinative act of pausing in it.

||||||||||||||||||||||||||||||||||||||||||||||||||||||||||||||||||||||||

Scientific research affirms what many have discovered without the benefit of a study—time spent in nature lowers stress levels, reduces anxiety, and improves overall well-being.[67]

Nature whispers an invitation to pause: Slow down. Breathe. Walk. Be renewed. When we step outside, we are not just moving into a different physical space—we are stepping into an environment that gifts us with connection to God in the deepest sense.

As with almost every element of soul care, finding life in the outdoors and being rejuvenated there doesn't have to be elaborate. Big things aren't always big. It could be:

» A quiet moment on a park bench
» Strolling through a wood
» Standing under a dark sky and looking up
» Listening to the sounds of nature—birds chirping, leaves rustling, water flowing
» Observing the clouds—what objects or animals do you see represented in them?
» Walking barefoot
» Sitting against a tree
» Laying in a hammock

It isn't just the presence of nature that restores; it is the determinative act of pausing in it. This is where burdens begin to feel lighter, and God's presence and voice become clearer.

---

67 Melanie Greaver Cordova, "Spending time in nature reduces stress, research finds," *Cornell Chronicle,* 25 Feb. 2020, https://news.cornell.edu/stories/2020/02/spending-time-nature-reduces-stress-research-finds.

For the incredible wonders that nature displays, it is no small wonder that we don't pause to take it in more. It would change our lives if we did.

In the Bible, God's creation is described as "good" (Genesis 1:31). Nature reveals His goodness, which is intrinsically linked to His holiness. The goodness of creation points to a holy and righteous Creator who loves us desperately and fully.

Romans 1:20: *"For since the creation of the world God's invisible qualities—his eternal power and divine nature—have been clearly seen, being understood from what has been made, so that people are without excuse."*

The intricate design of leaves and flowers, pine cones, mollusk shells, bleeding hearts and cockscombs, Venus flytrap and the cobra lily—the fact that snails hibernate and owls can rotate their heads 270 degrees—lungfish that can survive out of water for a year—eels that emit 750 volts of shock—each celebrate the majesty of the great Creative.[68]

Matthew 6:26-29: *"Look at the birds of the air; they do not sow or reap or store away in barns, and yet your heavenly Father feeds them. Are you not much more valuable than they? Can any one of you by worrying add a single hour to your life?"*

The natural symmetry of starfish and snowflakes and a butterfly's wings, the spiral of seashells, witness the harmony, splendor, and structure of God.

Psalm 19:1-4:

The heavens declare the glory of God;

---

68 Emily Shiffer, "The 45 Coolest Animals on the Planet Take Extreme Measures to Survive," *Popular Mechanics,* 19 Jan. 2023, https://www.popularmechanics.com/science/animals/g28857063/most-extreme-animals/.

the skies proclaim the work of his hands.
Day after day they pour forth speech;
night after night they reveal knowledge.
They have no speech, they use no words;
no sound is heard from them.
Yet their voice goes out into all the earth,
their words to the ends of the world.

Beyond its sheer beauty, nature reflects God's provision and care. The rain nourishes the earth, plants provide food and oxygen, animals live in carefully balanced habitats that sustain life. Every detail, from the migration of birds to the pollination of flowers, showcases His thoughtful design and invites humanity to draw closer to Him—to see Him there—to stand in awe of His greatness.

Psalm 104:24-25: *"How many are your works, LORD! In wisdom you made them all; the earth is full of your creatures. There is the sea, vast and spacious, teeming with creatures beyond number—living things both large and small."*

St. Augustine of Hippo once said:

> *Now, may our God be our hope. He Who made all things is better than all things. He Who made all beautiful things is more beautiful than all of them. Learn to love the Creator in His creature and the Maker in what He has made.*[69]

---

69 St. Augustine of Hippo, *Commentary on Psalm 39,* quoted in Dr. Robert Kurland, "God, Symmetry, and Beauty in Science: A Personal Perspective," *Magis Center,* 21 Oct. 2019, https://www.magiscenter.com/blog/god-symmetry-and-beauty-in-science-a-personal-perspective.

Ein Gedi

One of our regular touring sites when we visit the Holy Land is Ein Gedi. It's a nature reserve and oasis near the Dead Sea, known for its springs and biblical significance. It is the place where David hid in caves from King Saul (1 Samuel 24). Some of the Psalms are written from these caves as places of refuge for David.

The name Ein Gedi means "spring of the kid" (i.e., young goat).

Typically, we hike ten minutes or so into the reserve, enjoy the beautiful scenery, gather for a devotional from one of the Psalms, pray together, and make our way back to the bus toward our next destination. On one particular trip, our tour guide suggested we take the group further into the reserve where there was a beautiful waterfall that few touring groups get to see. He said the walk was about thirty minutes one way, but we had the time.

Let's go. Something different.

We navigated across small streams and on large and small boulders, along trails—it was easy going for the most part, a little scrambling here and there, but not bad. A dry hike, all in all. At some point, we could hear the sound of water in the distance, and if there was any tiredness in the group, the audio of running water washed the weariness away.

As Loren Eiseley is quoted as saying: "If there is magic on this planet, it is contained in water."[70] True that.

In another ten minutes, we saw it—fresh water tumbling over a limestone cliff into a clear pool—an escape from the

---

70 Loren Eiseley, *The Immense Journey* (New York: Random House, 1957), 15.

desert heat. Lush greenery surrounded by reeds, acacias, and other desert-adapted plants.

In times past, you would get out your Kodak and start snapping pictures of the site, whatever it was—the Grand Canyon, a redwood, a Dakota herd of bison, Pikes Peak, Lake Tahoe, the Apostle Islands, the Great Smokies, the Everglades, a sunflower field. But I noticed most of our group with their backs to the waterfall, phones held high to capture their own faces with the main attraction in the background. They were the headliner; nature was the supporting actor.

Somewhere along the way we forgot to fully honor the majesty of nature God put so much thought and heart into creating—and we made it about us instead. And our souls shriveled. We should pause more often to see the Creator in creation.

** Pause now, *return to the bullet point list (p. 269), and select a soul activity to practice being in the presence of the Creator God—or choose one from the list below.*

- » Pause to step outside in the early morning, when the air is crisp and the world feels freshly made.
- » Stand still for a moment and let the sunrise preach its quiet sermon—the new day is here. Rejoice and be glad in it.
- » Pause to watch the way a bird or butterfly flits from blossom to blossom. Notice the effortless beauty in its flight, the delicate strength in its wings, and remember that God's care extends to the smallest of creatures.
- » Take off your shoes and walk barefoot through the grass. Feel the cool beneath your feet, reminding you

that God formed you from dust and that you are loved with an everlasting love.

» Sit by a river or stream. Watch the steady, patient movement of the water as it carves paths that took years to form—and remember that God's work in you is slow, unstoppable, and sure.

» Lift your eyes to the tall trees. They do not strain or toil to reach the heavens; they simply grow, season by season, rooted in the place where God planted them.

Though it may not be remembered by anyone except early Boomers, Roy Rogers and Dale Evans sang the same song at the end of each episode of their outdoor-themed TV program, *The Roy Rogers Show,*[71] which aired from 1951 to 1957. As one website puts it: "The song is based on a song by Foy Willing of Riders of the Purple Sage, a group that backed Rogers in many of his Western films and appeared regularly on his 1940s radio program." The song and lyrics "represent a simpler time and a different set of values."[72]

One of the verses says:

Happy trails to you, it's great to say, "hello,"
And to share with you the trail we've come to know,
It started on the day that we met Jesus,
He came into our hearts and then he freed us,
For a life that's true, a happy trail to you.

||||||||||||||||||||||||||||||||||||||||||||||||||||||||||||||||||||

---

71 *The Roy Rogers Show,* Robert G. Walker et al. (June 9, 1957; New York, NY: NBC), Television.
72 "Happy Trails," lyrics, *Genius,* accessed June 19, 2025, https://genius.com/Roy-rogers-and-dale-evans-happy-trails-lyrics.

A Prayer to the Creator

Almighty Creator of Heaven and Earth,
I come before You with a heart full of praise, for
You alone are holy, righteous, and sovereign.
You spoke the world into existence, and by Your
power, all things are given life and sustained.
You are the source of all life and love. I come before You
with a humble heart, grateful for the gift of this day, for
the breath in my lungs and the light in my soul. You are
the Painter of the skies, the Sculptor of the mountains,
the Whisper in the wind, the Stillness in my heart.
In Your wisdom, You have woven the stars, and in
Your love, You formed me intricately before I was
a thought in my father's and mother's hearts.
Lord, I thank You for the gift of life, for the love
You have poured out through Jesus. Through His
sacrifice, You have redeemed me, and through His
resurrection, You have given me eternal hope.
Lord, in a world full of darkness, let me be a light.
Strengthen my faith, that I might fully trust in Your
promises, and give me boldness to share the gospel with
those who need You. You are my Refuge, my Strength,
my everlasting King. May Your will be done in my
life, and may all glory be Yours, now and forever.
Amen.

‖‖‖

PAUSE HACK: Take a few moments to enjoy nature. Go outside for a short walk. Sit by a window and watch the rain or snow fall.

||||||||||||||||||||||||||||||||||||||||||||||||||||||||||||||||||||

75-minute Soul Pause Application: Nature Prayer Walk

To embrace the beauty and import of today's soul care, plan a route where you can walk outdoors, a place where you can be fully present with Jesus. Hopefully, the weather is good as you plan your walk, but there is beauty in the rain if that's how the day turns out. God will meet you in unique ways in the rain as in the sunshine. Don't let inclement weather stop you.

Things to have with you:
» A Bible (paper or digital)
» Something to write with
» Your phone

You are encouraged to write in your book. By dedicating this time to soul care, you align your heart with God's peace and presence.

What Is a Prayer Walk and Why Should We Do It?

A prayer walk is a spiritual practice where you pray while walking, intentionally connecting with God and interceding for people, places, situations. It combines physical movement with prayer, helping you stay focused and engaged with God's presence while observing and praying within your surroundings.

Any time you engage in prayer, that's a success.

Tips for a successful prayer walk:

» Get a walking route in your mind before you head out.
» Ask God to guide your steps and prayers.
» Walk slowly and observe your surroundings in nature.
» Let what you see inspire you to pray.
» Ask God to bring His Kingdom to bear in the places you pass.
» Be thankful.

Let's walk.

Minutes 1-10: Prepare

To begin today, plan a route outdoors where you can walk and pray uninterrupted. As you begin that route, look up. Scan the sky. Ponder the greatness of God. Ask God to come into your time today with him. Spend these first minutes in this posture of prayer and "looking."

Minutes 10-20: Walk

Continue your route. Walk slowly. Observe things, people, settings all around you.

Pray silently for what comes into your view and heart as you walk. *(This can be uncomfortable at first if it's your first time. Push through the discomfort. You're doing fine. Just get in touch with God. Pray about what you see and what the Spirit brings to mind.)*

Minutes 20-30: Read

Pause for a moment and open your Bible to Psalm 19. Read the first two verses a few times.

Walk on—and reflect how nature reveals the presence of God. Pray prayers of thanksgiving for everything God has made.

Minutes 30-40: Worship

Pull up a worship song on your phone. For these next ten minutes, engage in worship as you walk. Thank God for the details of nature that you notice as you walk. Enjoy the presence of God. A song that speaks of nature would be a good selection here.

Minutes 40-55: Scripture and Reflection

Find a quiet place to sit. Read Genesis 1:31.

Reflect on how this reminds you of the goodness of God. Make notes of thoughts, emotions, and insights that come to mind.

Minutes 55-65: Surrender

What is on your heart right now? Ask God to remove any burdens you're carrying and to fill you with peace. Surrender any worries and cares to Him. Fully trust Him.

Minutes 65-75: Gratitude

Make your way to your ending destination. As you walk, spend the final moments just resting in God's presence. Thank Him for this time, for creation, for His faithfulness.

Be refreshed, knowing God is with you.

‖‖

Song:

"FOR THE BEAUTY OF THE EARTH"
by Folliott Sandford Pierpont (1864)[73]

---

73 Folliott Sandford Pierpoint, "For the Beauty of the Earth," 1864, public domain.

Chapter 12

The Gift of Now

"Gratitude is not only the greatest of virtues,
but the parent of all the others."
—Cicero[74]

I t was past midnight. The prison stank of sweat, mildew, and vermin. Rats boldly skittered from corner to corner. Chains clinked softly as prisoners shifted in their sleep.

In the deepest recesses of the stony prison where no moonlight could reach, two men sat—backs bruised, feet in stocks, wounds fresh from the last public beating: Paul and Silas.

---

74 Marcus Tullius Cicero, paraphrased as "*Gratus animus est...mater virtutum omnium reliquarum*" ("A grateful heart is not only the greatest virtue but the parent of all others"), Oratio Pro Cnæo Plancio, quoted in Jehiel Keeler Hoyt, Hoyt's New Cyclopedia of Practical Quotations (New York: Hoyt, 1922), 336–37.

They had done nothing wrong other than speak love and truth. Well, they *had* healed a slave girl tormented by an evil spirit and set her free. And for that, they were dragged into the open street to be accused, stripped, beaten and thrown in jail.

They could've been bitter.

They could've been angry.

Instead ... they *sang*.

Low at first. No more than a faint hum rising from Silas's cracked lips. Then Paul joined in, his voice rough but steady.

"I will sing of the LORD's great love forever; with my mouth I will make your faithfulness known through all generations. I will declare that your love stands firm forever, that you have established your faithfulness in heaven itself" (Psalm 89:1-2).

The song wasn't new to them. They had learned it as children at the feet of their teacher, Gamaliel. From an outward view, the words made no sense. Blood on their backs. Metal biting their ankles. Falsely accused. Behind bars. Uncertain futures.

And their play in that moment was to sing?

But the song grew louder and more sure—bouncing off the cold walls, threading through iron bars. Other prisoners stirred. Some knew the song; to others it was foreign. But they listened. And no one interrupted.

Something was happening. It wasn't just a song—it was worship in the face of cruel injustice. It was gratitude that refused to wait for the miracle to arrive. It was praise prior to the breakthrough.

Suddenly that low rumble. A nearly imperceptible vibration. Then a bit stronger. The ground began to shake. Walls groaned. Chains rattled. Stones cracked. The jail doors flew open. Every prisoner freed.

And... chaos. Just as the jailer was ready to take his own life for fear of losing all his prisoners, he heard Paul shout: "We're still here!" No one had escaped.

That night, the man who had guarded them for days found salvation in the love and grace they had been singing about. He bathed their wounds and fed them. And before the sun rose, he was baptized by them.

They expressed gratitude before they were freed.

They were thankful before they were delivered.

Their joy wasn't chained to circumstance. It was anchored in something far deeper.

Pausing to thank God in the middle of pain is a rebellious act of faith that invites the divine to break through.

Science Proves It

Okay. But take God out of it for a second.

The Greater Good Science Center in Berkeley, California, did a study on the practice of gratitude. Three hundred college students dealing with depression and anxiety were selected for the study. They were divided into three groups. The first group was asked to write a letter of gratitude to another person every week for three weeks. A second group was tasked to write about their recent negative experiences. The third group did not have any writing responsibility. Of the three groups, the participants who wrote letters of gratitude reported "significantly better mental health" twelve weeks after the study concluded. There are positive outcomes from gratitude, even when the gratitude is brief.[75]

That isn't all.

Studies show that when we are grateful, the brain stem releases a cocktail of feel-good chemicals—dopamine, serotonin, and oxytocin. Dopamine and oxytocin (the "cuddle hormone") make us feel good, and "because they feel good, we want more." When we reflect on and write down positive encouragements, our anterior cingulate cortex releases serotonin, the "happy molecule." "Serotonin enhances our mood . . . our willpower, and motivation."[76]

The more we activate these "gratitude" circuits, the stronger these neural pathways become.

A study by the International Journal of Workplace Health Management showed that gratitude was found to be a consistent predictor of:

» decreased exhaustion and cynicism
» a boost in proactive behaviors
» increased job satisfaction
» fewer illness-related absences.[77]

When we pause to appreciate who and what we already have, we shift from a mindset of scarcity to one of abundance. We begin to see that there is already so much good and beautiful in our lives. Gratitude roots us in enough-ness.

---

75 Joshua Brown and Joel Wong, "How Gratitude Changes You and Your Brain," *Greater Good Magazine,* 6 Jun. 2017, https://greatergood.berkeley.edu/article/item/how_gratitude_changes_you_and_your_brain.

76 Linda Roszak Burton, "The Neuroscience of Gratitude: What you need to know about the new neural knowledge," *Wharton Alumni Club, University of Pennsylvania,* accessed June 19, 2025, https://www. whartonhealthcare.org/the_neuroscience_of_gratitude.

77 Burton, "The Neuroscience of Gratitude.""

||||||||||||||||||||||||||||||||||||||||||||||||||||||||||||||||||||||||||||

Gratitude doesn't need to be dramatic. It just needs to be genuine.

||||||||||||||||||||||||||||||||||||||||||||||||||||||||||||||||||||||||||||

We don't stop striving—we just stop striving mindlessly.

Example: Paul

The apostle Paul was a master when it came to expressing gratitude. He includes it in nearly all of his New Testament writings.

To the church in Philippi, he said, "I thank my God every time I remember you. In all my prayers for all of you, I always pray with joy because of your partnership in the gospel from the first day until now" (Philippians 1:3-5).

We are reminded that showing gratitude for others can be a meaningful part of our prayer life.

To the church in Thessalonica: *"We always thank God for all of you and continually mention you in our prayers. We remember before our God and Father your work produced by faith, your labor prompted by love, and your endurance inspired by hope in our Lord Jesus Christ"* (1 Thessalonians 1:2-3).

This verse is an encouragement to appreciate others for their faithfulness and dedication.

To the church in Colossae: *"We always thank God, the Father of our Lord Jesus Christ, when we pray for you, because* *we have heard of your faith in Christ Jesus and of the love you have for all God's people"* (Colossians 1:3-4).

Gratitude for others is rooted in recognizing love and faith in action.

To the church in Rome: *"First, I thank my God through Jesus Christ for all of you, because your faith is proclaimed in all the world"* (Romans 1:8).

This scripture shows appreciation for the witness and testimony of others that strengthens the broader community.

To the church in Ephesus: *"For this reason, ever since I heard about your faith in the Lord Jesus and your love for all God's people, I have not stopped giving thanks for you, remembering you in my prayers"* (Ephesians 1:15-16).

The passage is an example of how gratitude for others should be often and constant.

To Philemon: *"I always thank my God as I remember you in my prayers, because I hear about your love for all his holy people and your faith in the Lord Jesus"* (Philemon 1:4-5).

It is a personal, warm expression of gratitude for an individual.

Grateful Ways

Gratitude isn't something we can do on the run. It demands we slow and look again—see what we have overlooked that is hiding in plain sight:

- » A meal shared
- » The kindness of a stranger
- » The beauty of family
- » Gainful employment

» Laughing with a group of friends
» Music that moves you

But wait. Go deeper, and by deeper, I mean go simpler yet:

» A bed to sleep on
» A roof over your head
» Shoes for your feet
» The smell of coffee
» The ability to turn on a faucet and get potable drinking water
» The feel of a hug
» Food on the table
» A hot shower

Simple things. The treasures of everyday life we so often miss as we're racing from one thing to the next. Gratitude doesn't need to be dramatic. It just needs to be genuine.

Here are a few ways to begin:

1) **Start and End Your Day with Gratitude.** Begin your morning with a humble, "God, I'm grateful for You"—for life, breath, for another opportunity.

    End your day by reflecting on three blessings from the day.

2) **Keep a Gratitude Journal.** Write down moments—big or small—that remind you of the goodness of God. This helps build awareness of how present and active God is in your life. These don't have to be profound—just real and honest.

    Gratitude journal categories might look something like this:

Small or large wins/ milestones today:	Current opportunities and what I'm learning from them:
Individuals I'm thankful for:	Significant assets in my life presently (health, relationships, monetary, mental):

3) **Praise Through Worship.** Worship is a powerful mode of gratitude. Don't just ask God for things— spend time thanking Him through song for who He is.

4) **Thank God Out Loud.** When you notice a blessing (a great parking spot, an answered prayer, peace in your heart, a healing, a problem solved), say, "Thank You, Lord," out loud. It builds a grateful mindset.

5) **Be Obedient.** Gratitude to God is shown by living according to His Word. Trusting and following His ways, even when it's hard, is a form of thankfulness.

6) **Give Generously.** God is the source of all you have. Generosity is not an action; it's a mindset and an attitude. Giving—through time, talents, and resources— is a way of saying, "Thank You, God, for what You've entrusted me with."

7) **Serve.** Service is a reflection of a thankful heart. When we bless others, we honor the God who has blessed us. We are blessed to be a blessing.

In a world that glorifies speed, achievement, and productivity, gratitude can seem passive. I'll admit—flashy, it ain't. But it's one of the most transformative forces we have. It has the potential to reshape our hearts and shift the atmosphere around us.

We should not take it for granted.

Seven _MORE_ Ways to Be Grateful (For Others)

1) **Say It (and Mean It).**
   Never underestimate a sincere "You're awesome." Make it specific—tell people what you're thankful for about them—especially the people you tend to take for granted. Often, these are the people closest to you. Let them know you see them.

2) **Send Notes of Appreciation.**
   A handwritten note, a kind text, an encouraging email can make someone feel deeply seen and appreciated.

3) **Pray for Them by Name.**
   Lift others up in prayer, thanking God for who they are and asking for blessing over their lives. Let them know you're praying—it will mean something special to them.

4) **Celebrate Their Wins.**
   Be excited about other people's successes. Be joyful with those who rejoice.

5) **Spend Quality Time.**
   Sometimes the best way to show appreciation is with your presence. When you're there, be fully there—no phone, no distractions.

6) **Speak Well.**
   Honor others behind their back. Be their cheerleader and advocate.

7) **Offer Help Without Being Asked.**

Step in when you notice someone could use a hand. Gratitude often looks like proactive kindness.

Gratitude is serious business. Imagine trying to find something to be grateful for when you end up in the worst possible situation you can envision. Others did...

» Inside the belly of a huge fish...
» Inside a prison of torture and death...
» Inside a body filled with disease...

Would you be thankful?

IIIIIIIIIIIIIIIIIIIIIIIIIIIIIIIIIIIIIIIIIIIIIIIIIIIIIIIIIIIIIIIIIIIIII

*Imagine you're in a dark, crowded theater, watching the drama unfold in a one-act play titled **JONAH INSIDE THE BELLY**...*

CHARACTER: Jonah

SETTING: The dark, claustrophobic interior of a great fish—wet, organic, echoing.

TIME: Three days have passed since Jonah was swallowed.

LIGHTING: One dim spotlight overhead with occasional pulses of blue for ocean movement. Shadows ripple across the set like waves.

[Lights up.]

(Jonah is hunched over, soaked and shivering. He's surrounded by a curved rib-like structure, slimy ropes of seaweed, and constant dripping overhead. There's a distant groan—like a deep-sea leviathan breathing.)

Jonah *(sharply, to the dark):*

You couldn't just let me drown, could You?
(He stands suddenly, slipping, agitated.)
I told them to throw me overboard!
I was ready!
The great storm crashing, waves tearing the sky in two—I thought *that* was justice for my disobedience.
But no. You sent *this* thing.
It swallowed me whole.
Now I'm alive . . . but inside some grotesque, gasping, gaping creature?
I'd rather be dead.
(He touches the wall of the great fish's belly—and recoils.)
This is not a tomb fit for a man.
This is a *waiting room.*
But for what? Another chance? Or just a longer, slower death?
(He laughs bitterly, his voice echoing in the cavern.)
You told me to go to Nineveh.
But I ran.
Fast and far.
I thought I could outrun Your voice.
(Pause. He begins to break, his voice softening.)
But even in my rebellion You chased me down.
Not to crush me, but to *catch* me.
(He kneels, trying to keep balance as the great fish turns. He steadies himself and breathes deeply—once. Twice. Then he looks up.)
You hear me. I know You do.
Even in here.

Even in this place no man should be.

You still hear me.

(He begins to pray, growing in emotion with each line.)

I offer myself to you. Thank you.

For not letting me die.

For not letting me go.

For holding me in this terrible, miraculous belly long enough for me to remember who I am.

And remember who You are.

Thank you.

(Another pause. A deep rumble. The belly begins to quake.)

If I ever walk free again—

I'll go.

I'll speak.

I'll obey.

No more running.

(Lights pulse brighter. The creature groans. The ground beneath him shifts. Jonah stands tall, now outside the cavern, facing the audience—his face upraised, thankful, and at peace.)

BLACKOUT.

[End Scene.]

Even inside the great fish, Jonah paused to pray a prayer of gratitude and give thanks to God: "I, with shouts of grateful praise, will sacrifice to you" (Jonah 2:9).

Jonah thanked God not for where he was at that moment, but for the answer he knew would come. Gratitude, even when he was in a pit, set Jonah apart—and when we offer it, it sets us apart, too.

Even for the Fleas

Gratitude expressed in the darkest places is a powerful act of faith. It has the profound quality of being able to coexist with pain. Gratitude doesn't overlook hardship; it radiates from inside of hardship. It doesn't suggest that we ignore our struggles; it calls us to remember that struggle is not the whole story.

One of the accounts I often heard while growing up was the story of Corrie and Betsie ten Boom. Their experience was made famous in the movie The Hiding Place.[78]

The ten Boom family were Dutch Christians living in the Netherlands during World War II. Their father created concealed spaces in their Amsterdam home where Jews could hide until they could covertly escape the terror of the Nazi regime. When the ten Booms were ultimately exposed by the German authorities, the sisters were sent to Ravensbrück, a notorious concentration camp for women.

Conditions there were horrific—over-crowding, starvation, and cruelty were daily realities. Their barracks were cramped and filthy. Worse, they found their beds infested with fleas.

Corrie, the younger of the sisters, became angry. She questioned how God could have allowed them to be in such an awful place. But Betsie had a different perspective.

One day, they read 1 Thessalonians 5:18 in their smuggled Bible: *"Give thanks in all circumstances; for this is God's will for you in Christ Jesus."*

---

78 James F. Collier, *The Hiding Place* (May 1975; Minneapolis, MN: World Wide Pictures).

Betsie insisted they thank God for everything—including the fleas. Corrie protested at first but eventually joined her sister in a whispered prayer of gratitude, even for that.

Weeks later, Corrie and Betsie discovered why the guards seldom came into their barracks, giving them the freedom to read the Bible aloud, pray, and minister to the other women. The guards refused to enter because of the fleas. Something that seemed unbearable on the surface was actually a divine protection.

Corrie later famously reflected: "There is no pit so deep, that God's love is not deeper still."[79]

Their story reminds us that gratitude isn't about liking everything—it's about trusting God in everything. Even when we don't understand it.

When we pause to be grateful "in spite of," we take back the narrative. We say, "Yes, this is hard. But there is still something here worth cherishing."

That shift in thinking and trusting is not small. In a world that is fond of turning the focus on self, gratitude whispers: "Stop and give thanks." And in that simple act of pausing, everything changes.

The One

They called themselves The Walkers.

Not because they preferred the designation—but because walking was all they had left. No home. No welcome mat. No meaningful touch. No loving relatives. Not sure where

79 Aubrynn Whitted, "Thankful for Fleas," *The Torchlighters,* 19 Nov. 2021, https://torchlighters.org/thankful-for-fleas/.

their next meal was coming from. Just the dusty road, their ragged clothing, and the disease that marked them as forever untouchable.

Ten of them, bound not by friendship so much as by a shared exile from society, from family, from life as they once knew it, dimly remembered.

But word travels. Even to the margins. A name. A man. A rumor of something—Someone miraculous—a Healer. What was his name? Jesus? Yes.

They paused to wait by the edge of the village. Not too close—the law wouldn't allow it. And when He finally appeared, they didn't beg with infirm hands, they cried out with pleading hearts: "Jesus, Master, have mercy on us!"

He didn't wave His hands over them or whisper a spell in their direction. He just said: "Go now. Show yourselves to the priests."

That's it?

But they went.

Step after uncertain step, and then—gradually, a tingling in their hands and feet—the sensation spreading across their skin. Something was changing.

Flesh whole. Spots gone. Pain replaced by—what is that unfamiliar thing we're feeling? Comfort? Relief? Joy?

Clean. All ten.

In that moment, they had a choice. Race ahead to reclaim their lives—or return to the Healer.

Nine ran forward. Only one turned back. The outsider among them. A Samaritan. The least likely to understand Jewish rituals, but perhaps the most likely to understand grace.

He ran—not to the priest—but to the Healer. He fell at Jesus's feet and poured himself out—not with another request, but with a grateful thank you.

Jesus, looking at him, said words that still reverberate through time: "Rise and go; your faith has made you well" (based on Luke 17:11-19).

Sometimes, the miracle is the body healing. But the greater miracle is in the heart that returns in thankfulness. Nine were healed. Only one, because of his gratitude and the grace of Jesus, was made whole.

Which would you rather have? Gratitude is the key.

Be Abnormal

There's little about gratitude that's normal. Not in a world where we're taught every day to grasp, grind, compare, and consume. Gratitude is unexpected. It's Godly rebellion. It sees mercy instead of mess.

In the Scriptures, the people of God gave thanks, not because life was easy, but because they knew God was faithful:

Hannah gave thanks for a son.

David praised in the wilderness.

Jonah offered gratitude from the belly of a fish.

Job blessed the name of the Lord with his world in ashes.

Mary sang a song of praise.

The one came back to say "thanks."

Jesus broke bread and gave thanks the night He was betrayed.

Paul sang from a prison cell.

There's nothing normal about that. These heroes beckon us to be abnormal by deciding to embrace gratitude.

Why not take a minute. Put the book down before turning the page. Look around your present setting. Find one thing or person to be thankful for. Gratitude doesn't need grand gestures. It just needs someone to pause and be grateful . . . right now.

A Prayer of Gratitude

Dear God,
Thank You for the gift of this day. For the breath
in my lungs, the beating of my heart, and the
still moments that remind me I am alive.
Thank You for Your love that surrounds me—
family, friends, and even strangers who show
kindness. Thank You for every challenge that has
shaped me, and every blessing that lifts me.
Thank You for the simple things—a warm meal, a
gentle act and sweet word, the beauty of nature, and
the peace that comes with pausing to hear You.
May I never take for granted Your light in my life.
Help me live with a heart that is grateful, to give more
than I take, and to see the good, even in the hard.
With humility and joy, I give You thanks.
Amen.

PAUSE HACK: Pick a wall ... a door ... a fridge ... any visible spot. Every day this week, grab a sticky note and write down one thing you're thankful for, big or small. Stick it there and leave it. Soon, that space becomes a colorful collage of gratitude.

||||||||||||||||||||||||||||||||||||||||||||||||||||||||||||||||||

1-Hour Soul Pause Application: Gratitude

It's okay if you're unable to complete the entire practice in one sitting. Give yourself permission to move at a pace that's gentle and sustainable—soul care isn't a race, but a journey of presence and grace.

To embrace the beauty and import of soul care, find a quiet and private place where you can be fully present with Jesus.

Things to have with you:

- » A Bible (paper or digital)
- » A paper journal to write on
- » A pen to write with

You are encouraged to write in your book. By dedicating this hour to soul care, you align your heart with God's peace and presence.

Minutes 1-5: Arrival and Intention

Find a quiet, cozy space. Sit comfortably and take three slow, grounding breaths.

Tell God your intention for this hour. For instance: "I open myself to gratitude. Soften my heart and open my senses to be thankful for what You've given."

Read Psalm 100.

Minutes 5-15: Gratitude Body Scan
Read Psalm 139:13-14
Read 1 Corinthians 6:19-20
Close your eyes and bring attention to the body God has created. Move through a mental scan of your body and give thanks to God for each part of you—top to bottom.
Sense appreciation for your own body—not for how it looks, but for what it allows you to do.

Minutes 15-30: Gratitude Journaling
In a notebook (or in the space provided below), respond to the following prompts. Don't overthink—just write what comes to mind.
Three good things from this week.
A person you're grateful for—and why.
A challenge you faced recently that taught you something.
Something small that brings you joy (a smell, a sound, a memory).
One of your gifts/talents that you're grateful for.
Give thanks for each one above.

Minutes 30-40: Gratitude Walk or Movement
Take a short walk. Move slowly and notice things around you that you can easily be thankful for. Express that gratitude to God. Let each step or movement become a prayer of thanks.

Minutes 40-55: Letter of Gratitude (Sent or Unsent)
With the journal you brought, write a letter to someone who has made your life better. Be detailed.

>> What did they do for you?
>> How did it affect your life?
>> What do you wish they knew about what they did?

You don't have to send the letter, but do write it. This is about expressing emotion and feeling.

Optional: Text or email a quick "thank you" to someone God brought to your mind during this section.

Minutes 55-60: Reflection
Return to your initial quiet space.

Write one final sentence: *"Right now I am thankful for*

_____*."*

Hold that thought in your heart and head. Pray a closing prayer of gratitude to God.

(NOTE: Consider doing this once a week as a personal reset.)

"Beloved, I pray that all may go well with you and that you may be in good health, as it goes well with your soul."
—3 John 2 (ESV)

Song:

"HOLY, HOLY, HOLY"
by Reginald Heber (1826)[80]

---

80 Reginald Heber, "Holy, Holy, Holy," 1826, public domain.

Chapter 13

When the Ground Shifts Beneath You

"When you're going through hell, keep going."
—Attributed to Winston Churchill

There's a strange kind of magic in ordinary happiness. Life is good—not extraordinary or cinematic or anything—but comfortably good. You don't realize you're living in it until something rips it away.

I'm a frequent member at the gym. If nothing else, the environment is a stress reliever, and it at least helps me *imagine* I'm in some livable kind of shape. It's amazing the tricks your mind gives permission to play on you.

It was springtime, 2022. I spent my usual forty-five minutes at Planet Fitness with my earbuds blasting away in my head, lifting some weights, doing some cardio, chowing down on a tasteless protein bar, and chasing it with some green sludge the internet tells me I'm supposed to drink to be healthy. It was a normal late afternoon. When I arrived home, I noticed I had overexerted my right shoulder. This happens from time to time during workouts, when I subconsciously try to compete with the thirty-year-old dude with 6 percent body fat standing next to me, and I end up picking up a weight ten pounds too heavy just to prove to some stranger that I can—as if he's actually watching—and then acting like it didn't hurt when I was done. Well, it did hurt on this day.

As many have said, *"Pride goeth before a fall . . . which explains why I trip so much."*

I came to a quick and wise conclusion that I needed to lay off the heavier stuff until my body could heal itself—and then be more careful in future.

The next several weeks held regular workout days—except the gnawing pain in my shoulder continued. It wasn't debilitating; it was just a dull thud, except over time it had migrated to my back and down my right arm as well. Still, I employed a grin-and-bear-it philosophy over the course of those weeks. It will go away. It always does. Summer was approaching and things get worked out on their own in the summer.

Our church board had granted us a three-month sabbatical that year, and Joelene and I were looking forward to the time away. What a gift from our leadership! During this period of rest and renewal we took the opportunity to travel. Every time I picked up a piece of luggage, it would aggravate that ache in my shoulder and arm. I couldn't wear a backpack for more than an hour or two before having to take it off and carry it with my left hand. I determined to make some visits to the chiropractor when I returned home. Get this thing figured out.

We have friends—brothers—who are chiropractors, and I knew I was in good hands, not only physically, but relationally. They care about me. It was fall now—six months since the discomfort first showed up. The doc worked on me for another several weeks and it seemed on certain days to improve, but he finally said, *"I don't know that we're making the kind of progress I would like to see. Let's get an X-ray. See what's going on in there."* I went the next day.

That night was the November birthday of one of our team members. He had reached out to the "guys" on the team to hit a late night movie premier together as part of his celebration. I'm asked to do that kind of thing every now and then by the staff. I know they invite the senior guy out of honor—to be nice—which I appreciate. Sometimes I decline and let the youngsters have their fun, but on this night I decided to tag along and be with the team. The movie started at 9 p.m. I'm usually deep in REM sleep and into my fourth dream by that time, but ...

We were standing in the lobby theater waiting on our popcorn when I got a text. It was the chiro brothers. *Call us.*

"*Hello.*"

"*Hey.*"

"Where are you right now?" Seemed like an odd question to ask me at 8:30 at night.

"I'm at Tinseltown waiting to see a movie with some of the team."

"OK. We're on our way to see you."

"Now? Both of you?"

"Yes. We're driving now. We can be there in fifteen minutes."

There is that ominous moment when you feel the ground shifting beneath your feet. There comes a dizziness. Some half-truth flashes across your brain. You can't quite grab on to it; it's there and then all of a sudden, it fades a bit. You try to wish it all the way away, but it lingers in the dark in the back of your mind where you can't see it outright, but you know it's still there.

They arrived and we retreated to a corner of the theater lobby. There was little to no introduction.

"There's a mass."

Silence.

"It's large. We're so sorry. You need to get a biopsy."

The words were said with as much compassion and care as one can say such words—to this day I'm thankful for these good friends—but the news was a sledgehammer to my spirit. There might have been more words spoken; I don't recall. Mass. Large. Biopsy. Those I remember. They aren't words you want to hear strung together in the same sentence and lobbed your direction. They laid their hands on me right there in the lobby and prayed for me.

During the next four weeks I saw more doctors than I had in sixty years of living. They told me it could be a shadow. It could be benign. It could be "something else." I got the biopsy.

IIIIIIIIIIIIIIIIIIIIIIIIIIIIIIIIIIIIIIIIIIIIIIIIIIIIIIIIIIIIIIIIIIIIIIIIIIIIIIIIIIIIIII

Life doesn't announce its storms. It just drops them into your hands and waits to see if you'll catch them, or if you'll be crushed by them.

IIIIIIIIIIIIIIIIIIIIIIIIIIIIIIIIIIIIIIIIIIIIIIIIIIIIIIIIIIIIIIIIIIIIIIIIIIIIIIIIIIIIIII

We were in Minneapolis at the Mall of America in the LEGO store when my phone rang. It's always the phone, isn't it? A sharp chime, cutting through the calm. It was the doctor. Her voice was steady—too steady. The kind of voice that had practiced this conversation a hundred times before.

"We have your results."

A pause. A breath. A prayer. *Please, God.*

"I know this isn't what you want to hear, and it isn't what I want to tell you—but it's cancer."

The word felt alien in my ear, like it belonged to someone else's story. And yet, it was mine. A handful of syllables that rearrange your world—and there was that sledgehammer again. One moment I'm looking at a LEGO box with the Statue of Liberty in two thousand pieces, the next moment I'm floating outside my body, my heart pounding out a strange and foreign rhythm. Disbelief.

"We have some meetings scheduled with your oncologist to put together a plan as soon as you get back."

I have an oncologist? Life doesn't announce its storms. It just drops them into your hands and waits to see if you'll catch them, or if you'll be crushed by them.

Joelene and I walked to the food court and sat at a little table to FaceTime our kids. I can't remember much of what was said in that conversation—I was shell-shocked by the news. I remember tears. We agreed together as a family that we were going to put our hope in Jesus. Joelene said we were going to buy a recliner for the living room. It didn't strike me at the time that she was already wondering what the future might look like. I know that she, like me, was afraid.

The disease had originated in my lymph nodes and spread through my upper back and even attacked parts of my spine. The doctor said it was large and aggressive and proposed a plan to treat it. Over the course of the next months, I lay in bed every night with the phone next to my ear, letting Jesus speak to me through song. Two songs in particular:

"The Goodness of God" by Bethel Music—I loved hearing CeCe Winans sing it. One of the verses says:

I love Your voice, You have led me through the fire,
In the darkest night You are close like no other.
I've known You as a Father, I've known you as a friend.[81]

81 CeCe Winans, vocalist, "Goodness of God" by Ben Fielding, Brian Johnson, Edmond Martin Cash, Jason ingram, and Jenn Johnson, 2021, track 12 on *Believe for It*, Bethel Music Publishing.

And ... "Firm Foundation (He Won't)" by Maverick City Music—Cody Carnes's version. The bridge reads:

Rain came, wind blew, my house was built on You.
I'm safe with You, I'm gonna make it through.[82]

Every line a personal, whispered prayer, reminding me that God was near ... and faithful ... and good ... and *enough*. Each line a promise to see me through. I trust You, God. Like I have for the past sixty years. It feels a little more desperate this time, but ... You're my hope. You're my peace. You're my strength. You're my joy. You're my everything.

Sometimes the ground shifts—life hits the brakes—whether you want it or not, and typically you don't. But those forced moments can be ridiculously powerful. They can come in a wide variety of ways:

» A physical issue
» A mental health struggle
» A relational difficulty or break-up
» A divorce
» The loss of someone close to you
» Emotional exhaustion or breakdown
» Career or financial setback
» Burnout
» Mid-life crisis
» Empty nest syndrome
» Taking on caregiving responsibilities

---

82 Cody Carnes, vocalist, "Firm Foundation" by Maverick City Music, 2023, track 4 on *Firm Foundation (Live)*, Sparrow Records.

Lots of things can force you to press pause on life. When that happens, what do you do? You need a Pause Plan. Following is a plan I put into place when the unexpected came into my own life.

If you're in an unexpected season, try it—and watch God meet you in the middle of your storm.

A Nine-Step Pause Plan

1) **Pause to breathe.** I'm not kidding. Sounds cliché. But seriously—breathe. You don't need to solve it all in twenty-four hours. Just acknowledge the deep need to pause.

2) **Pause to give yourself permission to feel.** It's okay to grieve, it's okay to feel lost, and it's okay to be frustrated or confused. Certain wounds need time. Don't rush to "fix" yourself. Feel without judgment. That's how it moves through you instead of getting you stuck.

3) **Pause to surrender to the will of God.** Trust that everything happens for a reason and is meant to bring glory to God and is for your ultimate good, even if you don't understand it right now.

   Neither you nor your situation were a surprise to God, which means there's already a plan in progress. Take some time to memorize scriptures that speak to your situation. Repeat them over and over to yourself—verses that remind you of God's divine love, deliverance, protection, peace, presence, and healing.

   Challenges can be used as occasions to come closer to God if we'll surrender to Him.

4) **Pause to get curious.** Ask yourself: "Why now?" And, "What is my soul meant to learn from this?" Maybe something in your life needs to stop so something else can start. Maybe God is trying to tell you to rest before the next climb.

This might be a season that forces you to get the much-needed rest you require. You'd never otherwise take advantage of that unless God made you lie down. A shift in perspective is often what we need during circumstances like these.

Time doesn't automatically heal everything, but time and curiosity can be a teacher. What is time teaching you? What have you been too busy to notice? A forced pause often helps you see it more clearly.

5) **Pause to shift the narrative.** Instead of "I'm lost," try: "I'm recalibrating." Words matter. The story you tell yourself ultimately becomes your reality.

This is where putting feelings into words can be healing. I began to journal my own journey during my season of treatments. What was God saying? What scriptures came to mind? Don't push those sensations away. That's the Holy Spirit speaking. Record them, even if they seem insignificant at the time. Small steps are still steps.

You will look back and see the voice and timely hand of God, I promise you.

6) **Pause to find small anchors in the chaos.** Simple routines can become powerful: Regular morning coffee or tea, devotional time, short walks, meditation on

Scripture, a time of prayer, pausing to listen—all help create stability in your life.

Ask yourself: "What good can possibly come from this challenge?" It's a good question to grapple with. There's always a God answer waiting for you.

7) **Pause to be grateful.** We spent a whole chapter on this, but it bears repeating. Being grateful sounds so strange when you're walking through dark spaces, but giving thanks for past blessings keeps us centered on God, no matter how small those blessings may be. Being in a tempest doesn't mean you have walked outside the favor of God. Gratitude doesn't cancel out pain, but acknowledging good things can bring moments of relief that are healing to your soul.

8) **Pause to lean on someone.** You don't have to walk this valley alone. There are people who care about you. If you need to seek professional help, don't hesitate. There's beauty and strength in realizing when you need extra support and then having the humility to act on it.

You can also turn that around. Don't just lean into your own leaning. Find another who is leaning and offer to help them. Compassion lifts the soul. Serving others brings healing and perspective to your pain. There's almost always someone who has it worse than you.

9) **Pause with patience, faith, and hope.** Healing and recovery don't follow a schedule. There's no prescriptive "right way" to navigate through tragedy and

difficulty. Take it one moment at a time. Some days will be harder than others. That's OK. Trust God's timing. **Remember that seasons of hardship are usually that—seasons.** In time, this will pass. Wait patiently. Have faith in your Creator God. Keep hope alive. Believe that joy, renewal, and greater spiritual strength will emerge on the other side of the trial, if not before.

What a Forced Pause Taught Me

Things change when deep, personal crisis hits home. What you think about changes. What you dream about changes. How you view the future changes. The way you respond to people changes. How you sing and pray and laugh and dance changes. Everything . . . changes.

It did for me.

When something comes into your life that forces you to pause, your humanity comes into sharper focus.

As I paid greater attention to myself, I saw a deeper purpose God was trying to reveal for my life—a greater connection to the One who loves me. A deeper appreciation for small things. I began to see the people around me through a new lens: people Jesus really loves. Greater patience for the detours of life. A more accurate spotlight on first-world problems that I had elevated to must-solve-today crises.

A greater understanding began to grow in me that God was working as much on my spiritual insides as He was on my body. More. He was performing scans on my soul that an MRI could never detect. There was cultivated in me a desire to have more of Jesus. To be more like Him. To listen more closely. To invite Him to work on the parts of me that couldn't be seen with the naked eye. How tragic to navigate all the way through life—see great sights, live in relative comfort, eat, drink, and be merry, and enjoy a great set of family and friends—but end up with a soul that isn't redeemed by God.

"What good will it do someone if he gains the whole world but forfeits his life?" (Matthew 16:26, CJB)

When something comes into your life that forces you to pause, your humanity comes into sharper focus. Life here is not forever: "You are a mist that appears for a little while and then vanishes" (James 4:14).

My outer shell is deteriorating . . . fast. So is yours. Let's blame it on those first two in the garden. Works for me. Gravity, in multiple ways, is not my friend. But there's a world beyond this one that is extravagantly beautiful. He does not leave me here. He's preparing a place for me there.

I'm convinced now that the most important kind of healing isn't physical. Does God care about that? Yes. *Jehovah Rapha*, my Healer, sees and cares about my body, but I no longer believe my physical issue is His deepest concern. He knew what I would be navigating before it ever reached my body, and He permitted something in my life to draw me nearer. That's what all this is for—life, I mean. Whatever brings me more of Jesus.

"My grace is sufficient for you, for my power is made perfect in weakness." Therefore I will boast all the more gladly about my weaknesses, so that Christ's power may rest on me. That is why, for Christ's sake,

I delight in weaknesses, in insults, in hardships, in persecutions, in difficulties. For when I am weak, then I am strong. —2 Corinthians 12:9-10

"*Being confident of this very thing, that he who began a good work in you will perfect it until the day of Jesus Christ*" (Philippians 1:6).

That's my hope and desire—to be more like Jesus—whatever it takes. Whatever? Yes.

I wish there was a formula in Scripture I could frame and hang on the wall that would guarantee everything would work out my way if I simply followed these ten rules for life. No such formula exists. I had to "let go and let God" and affirm that He holds the big world and my relatively small life in His hands and He is worthy of my trust and devotion—my faith—my all.

|||||||||||||||||||||||||||||||||||||||||||||||||||||||||||||||||||||||||||||||||||||

Even bad days are better than no days.

|||||||||||||||||||||||||||||||||||||||||||||||||||||||||||||||||||||||||||||||||||||

Before this came into my life, I thought I was a stronger person. I realized during this journey that I'm not as Herculean as I let on. I'm dependent. Desperately so. I need people. I need friends and family. I need God and His deep well of mercy—all the time.

As 1 Corinthians 15:10 (ESV) says, "His grace toward me is not in vain."

During this season of pausing, for the first time in my life, I understood what fear smells like. It doesn't smell pleasant. I understood that life is not always wrapped up in a pretty package with a nice bow on top. Pain is part of life. I also learned what peace and contentment smell like. They smell pretty amazing. And they're promised. I've felt the raging inferno up close and personal, and I know the reality of the "fourth man" in the fire. He is faithful and true. I'll make it through, one way or another, and still have Jesus on the other side. He never fails.

"Be strong and courageous. Do not fear or be in dread of them, for it is the LORD your God who goes with you. He will not leave you or forsake you" (Deuteronomy 31:6, ESV).

During my forced pause, I began to live more in the truth of Philippians 1:21: "For to me, to live is Christ and to die is gain." I don't fear death anymore—and I know that each day is a gift from the Creator. Even bad days are better than no days.

The Rest of the Story

Several months post-diagnosis—after multiple chemotherapy/immunotherapy treatments . . . medications . . . shots . . . appointments . . . loss of my hair/cyebrows/eyelashes—I underwent a PET scan that revealed the cancer was in remission. As of this writing, it still is.

Thanks be to God. He gets 100 percent of the praise for that work. Not merely a survivor of cancer, but a victor through Jesus Christ.

Praise the LORD, my soul;
all my inmost being, praise his holy name.
Praise the LORD, my soul,
and forget not all his benefits—
who forgives all your sins
and heals all your diseases,
who redeems your life from the pit
and crowns you with love and compassion,
who satisfies your desires with good things
so that your youth is renewed like the eagle's.
—Psalm 103:1-5

I know that not everyone's story turns out like mine, but God directs our steps no matter who we are. He has a plan and a purpose. And irrespective of what happens, man, is He ever good!

"Trust in the LORD with all your heart and don't lean on your own understanding; in all your ways submit to him, and he will make your path straight" (Proverbs 3:5-6).

"He has made everything beautiful in its time" (Ecclesiastes 3:11).

Amen. Selah.

A Prayer When Hard Times Come

Dear Father,
In this moment of struggle, I come before You with a
heavy heart. The burdens I carry feel too great, and the
path ahead seems uncertain. But I know You are my
refuge and strength, a present help in time of trouble.
Lord, I trust You. When my spirit feels weak, lift me. When
my heart is weary, refresh me. When doubts creep in,
remind me of Your unconditional love. I believe that even
in my trials, You are working all things for my good.
Give me the courage to face each day with faith,
knowing You walk beside me. Fill me with Your peace
that surpasses understanding. Help me to hold onto
hope, even when the storm rages around me.
I surrender my worries, my fears, and my pain
to You. Let Your will be done in my life and
guide me in the path that You provide.
Thank You, Lord, for never leaving me or forsaking
me. I place my faith in You, now and forever.
Amen.

‖‖‖

PAUSE HACK: Before getting out of bed/before going to bed, think of three things you're grateful for.

‖‖‖

1-Hour Soul Care Application: Trusting God

It's okay if you're unable to complete the entire practice in one sitting. Give yourself permission to move at a pace that's gentle and sustainable—soul care isn't a race, but a journey of presence and grace.

To embrace the beauty and import of soul care, find a quiet and private place where you can be fully present with Jesus.

Things to have with you:

» A Bible (paper or digital)
» Something to write with
» Your phone

You are encouraged to write in your book. By dedicating this hour to soul care, you align your heart with God's peace and presence.

Minutes 1-5: Presence

When a forced pause comes into a life, one of the first go-tos we might think of is Job in the Bible. Nobody experienced more unexpected and sudden turns than Job.

Meditate on Job 1:21: "The LORD gave, and the LORD has taken away; blessed be the name of the LORD."

You are in God's presence right now. Find a quiet place and invite God to come into your time this hour as you pray.

Minutes 5-15: Strengthen

God has already been faithful to you in your past. Reflect on those times.

Make a mental or written gratitude list. Run through it and be thankful. This will serve to strengthen your spirit.

Minutes 15-35: Reflect

Read these scriptures: Job 1:6-12; Job 2:7-10; Job 42:10-12.
Reflect on Job's:
1) Suffering
2) Questioning
3) Restoration
Ask yourself:
What thing or things in life are overwhelming me right now—they feel like "too much?" Maybe you're on the edge—even on the verge of breaking. Write those below.

_____

_____

_____

_____

_____

_____

As you review the lines above, have you been questioning God about any of those things?

A lament is not just an expression of sorrow. It is a prayer in our pain that leads to trust in God, believing in the promises of God for us.

Write your own Job-like lament below. It's OK. Be honest with yourself. God already knows your heart. Just tell Him how you feel. Acknowledge any doubt or pain and hurt.

_____

_____

_____

_____

_____

_____

Minutes 35-50: Release

Release means laying something down and letting something go.

What do you believe about the faithfulness of God?

Look up and read these scriptures that focus on His miracle-working power:

» Jeremiah 32:27
» Mark 11:24
» Job 19:25

Read and declare these verses OUT LOUD—affirm your trust in God.

Now... lay those needs that you wrote earlier before God. Pray with faith about each of them. Remember that faith is not about seeing; it's about trusting.

Release each of them to God. Believe that He can do all things.

Minutes 50-60: Expectation

"You have heard of Job's perseverance and have seen what the Lord finally brought about. The Lord is full of compassion and mercy" (James 5:11).

Worship with a song of trust on your phone.

Closing moment: *"After Job had prayed for his friends, the LORD restored his fortunes and gave him twice as much as he had before"* (Job 42:10).

Ask yourself:

How will I trust God moving forward?

Who, besides me, is walking through something difficult? How can I encourage them today?

Finish your time with a simple prayer of surrender: "Lord, I don't understand everything, but I trust You. Give me strength to endure, faith to believe, and love to share. Amen."

"Beloved, I pray that all may go well with you and that you may be in good health, as it goes well with your soul."
—3 John 2 (ESV)

SONG:

" 'TIS SO SWEET TO TRUST IN JESUS"
by Louisa M. R. Stead (1882)[83]

---

83 Louisa M. R. Stead, "'Tis So Sweet to Trust in Jesus," 1882, public domain.

Rebel Soul
Postscript

Kevin had spent most of his life sprinting through his days like a soldier on autopilot—phone buzzing, calendar packed, always pushing, always performing. He didn't question the pace; it was just the way the world worked. In a culture that equates exhaustion with importance, busyness had become his identity. Beneath the momentum was the kind of fatigue that sleep couldn't solve—the soul-deep weariness of someone who had forgotten how to *be*.

One evening late, as he hurried home from work, he found himself caught in traffic. Frustrated, he gripped the steering wheel, drumming his fingers impatiently. But then, something caught his eye—a defiant sunset sprawling across the sky in wild strokes of lavender and fire. A protest against the pace.

For the first time in a long time, Kevin let go of the rush. He didn't really know why he gave in to the urge, but he turned off the music, pulled to the side of the road, took a deep breath, and simply watched until the colors faded to gray. The beauty of the moment wasn't in accomplishing anything in particular or progressing forward. It was in the pausing itself.

That day became a catalyst for future rebellion.

The next morning, he sipped his hot tea a little slower instead of drinking it on the run. When his friend called to talk that day, he really listened, without mentally planning his response in order to finish the conversation and move on. At lunchtime, he walked outdoors and let himself enjoy the warmth of the sun on his skin instead of cramming the hoagie down his throat in between answering emails. He soaked in the joy of laughter with a coworker, appreciated the squirrel that dashed across his path on the afternoon errand run, and was more conscious of the stillness of night before bed.

Seemingly tiny revolutions, but he started naming the pauses not as wasted time, but as sacred resistance. He called them Selahs—like in the Psalms. Essential breaks in the noise.

Kevin began to grasp that in a world that screams "go faster," choosing stillness is radical. Presence is protest.

Kevin. That's me. And this is my daily rebellion.

Full Circle

The last time I was in Waupaca, Wisconsin, the silent prayer retreat did not bring any brand-new revelations... no kayak dumps... no loss of iPhone or sandals or Bible... no audible voice—only more head down, more slow walking, more silence, more being with Jesus. Maybe an extra nap or two.

Our whole church staff team continues to absorb and relish the quarterly soul-care sessions and guides provided for them.

We are learning that there come moments when the soul whispers what the body refuses to acknowledge: You need to pause. Not just the kind of pause that's attached to a good nap, but the kind of restorative pause where Jesus comes in the room and makes everything better—the kind of pause that reaches into the manic places of the heart and encourages us to really live, not merely exist.

Jesus was never hurried, yet He finished all He needed to do. He withdrew to hushed places, not out of weakness, but out of wisdom. He knew that pausing to care for His soul was not a luxury. It was a necessity. Even Jesus.

He said: *"Come to Me, all who are weary and burdened, and I will give you rest"* (Matthew 11:28).

That "all" includes you. You are not exempt from caring for your soul. When we pause to sit with Jesus, our souls exhale. The weight we carry, at times heavy and even unnoticed, begins to lift—and we realize there is another way to live. A better way.

So—pause.

Pause—to know who Shepherds your path.

Pause—to recognize you are God's favorite creation.
Pause—to abide with Jesus.
Pause—to listen to His voice.
Pause—to surrender every day.
Pause—to be filled with His Spirit.
Pause—to sabbath and remember.
Pause—to connect with others.
Pause—to be grateful.

And as you go, may you remember that to care for your soul in a world that demands constant output is the best kind of rebellion.

Appendix

Christian practices for nurturing the soul are as diverse as they are divine. By engaging in one or more of these, you can experience profound spiritual growth and a closer relationship with God. These practices serve as a roadmap for a fulfilling and God-focused life, guiding the soul that has learned how to pause.

"ANYTIME" SOUL-CARE REBELLION

Morning: Set the Tone for the Day
1) Quiet Reflection (5-10 minutes)
   » Sit in a quiet space. Express gratitude for the day ahead.
   » Ask yourself, "What do I hope for today?" or "What is one thing I can do to stay connected to God?"
2) Spiritual Practice (5-15 minutes)
   » Prayer, Scripture reading, meditating on a passage.
   » Set an intention for the day around a fruit of the Spirit, such as kindness, patience, or peace.
3) Movement (10-20 minutes)
   » A short walk can awaken your body and clear your mind.
   » As you move, focus on being present with Jesus.

Midday: Recharge and Realign
1) Pause and Breathe (2-5 minutes)
   » Step away from work or responsibilities for a moment. Check in with Jesus—be in touch with your thoughts and feelings.
   » Acknowledge any stress and let it go.
2) Nurture Connection (5-10 minutes)
   » Reach out to someone you care about for a brief, meaningful conversation that brings life.
   » Alternatively, spend time journaling about what's on your heart or mind.
3) Fuel Yourself (10-20 minutes)

» Eat a nutritious meal or snack, and savor it slowly.
» Avoid distractions like screens during this time.

Evening: Reflect and Unwind
1) Reflection and Gratitude (5-10 minutes)
   » Write in a journal or think about three things you were grateful for that day.
   » Reflect on what went well and where you'd like to grow tomorrow.
2) Spiritual or Relaxation Practice (10-20 minutes)
   » Engage in calming activities like reading, prayer, meditation, listening to peaceful music, being with good friends.
   » If needed, offer forgiveness to yourself or others for anything that is unresolved.
3) Wind Down for Rest
   » Avoid screens at least thirty minutes before bed.
   » Create a peace-filled nighttime routine like dimming the lights, sipping tea, or reading something uplifting.

Weekly/Monthly Pauses
» *Spend Time in Nature:* Go for a hike, walk on the beach, or sit in a park. Nature has a restorative effect.
» *Community Connection:* Attend a group or service that aligns with your spiritual values.
» *Creative Expression:* Paint, write, play music, or engage in any creative activity that nourishes your soul.

» *Extended Reflection:* Dedicate longer periods (e.g., an hour or a half-day) to reflection, silence, intentional lengthier pauses.

Tips for Deepening a Prayer Life

1) *Establish a Routine:* Set aside dedicated times each day—such as morning devotions or evening reflection.
2) *Incorporate Scripture:* Use Bible passages to guide your prayers, allowing God's Word to shape your petitions and praises.
3) *Create a Sacred Space:* Designate a quiet, comfortable place for soul care to minimize distractions and create a sense of reverence.

How to Engage with Scripture

1) *Follow a Bible Reading Plan to systematically explore the chapters of the Bible.*
   5x5x5 Plan: Navigators—https://www.navigators.org/wp-content/uploads/2021/12/navigators-5x5x5-new-testament-bible-reading-plan.pdf
   YouVersion: https://www.bible.com/reading-plans
   Bible Project: https://bibleproject.com/reading-plans/
   The Bible in 90 Days (CSB): https://csbible.com/wp-content/uploads/2018/01/CSB90-DayReading-Plan.pdf
2) *Practice Lectio Divina:* This ancient practice involves reading a passage slowly, meditating on its message, praying for understanding, and contemplating its application.

3) *Journal Your Reflections:* Write down insights that can deepen your engagement with the text and record impressions you hear from the Holy Spirit.
4) *Engage in S.O.A.P.* = Scripture/Observation/Application/Prayer: https://jrnychurch.com/soap

Worship and Sacraments
1) *Music and Singing:* Engage with hymns and contemporary worship songs that resonate with your spiritual journey.
2) *The Lord's Supper:* Participate in communion to reflect on Christ's sacrifice and express gratitude.
3) *Fellowship:* Connect with others in your faith community to share experiences and offer mutual encouragement.

Fasting
1) *Start Small:* Begin with a short fast, such as skipping one meal, and gradually increase the duration.
Types of fasts: https://jrnychurch.com/fast/
2) *Replace with Prayer:* Use the time saved from fasting to pray or meditate on Scripture.
3) *Simplify Your Life:* Identify and remove distractions or possessions that hinder your spiritual growth.

Acts of Service
1) *Volunteer Locally:* Find opportunities in your community to serve, such as food banks or shelters.

2) *Practice Everyday Kindness:* Look for simple ways to help others, like running errands for a neighbor.

3) *Support a Mission:* Contribute to or participate in mission work to share God's love globally.

Solitude and Silence

1) *Set Aside Time:* Dedicate a few minutes daily to sit quietly in God's presence.
   For instance: https://www.24-7prayer.com/

2) *Go on Retreat:* Attend a spiritual retreat to disconnect from daily life and focus on your faith.

3) *Practice Listening Prayer:* Instead of speaking, listen for God's voice in your heart and mind.

Gratitude and Thanksgiving

1) *Keep a Gratitude Journal:* Write down daily blessings to remind yourself of God's goodness.

2) *Express Thanks to Others:* Make encouragement a regular part of your walk.

3) *Celebrate God's Gifts:* Share your blessings with others through testimonies and acts of kindness.

FOLLOW THE LEADER

STAY CONNECTED

f facebook.com/TheArtofAvail   @theartofavail   △ AVAIL

AVAIL
PODCAST

LISTEN WHEREVER YOU GET YOUR PODCASTS
AVAIL LEADERSHIP PODCAST

www.ingramcontent.com/pod-product-compliance
Lightning Source LLC
Chambersburg PA
CBHW070527090426
42735CB00013B/2889